DOT MARKERS

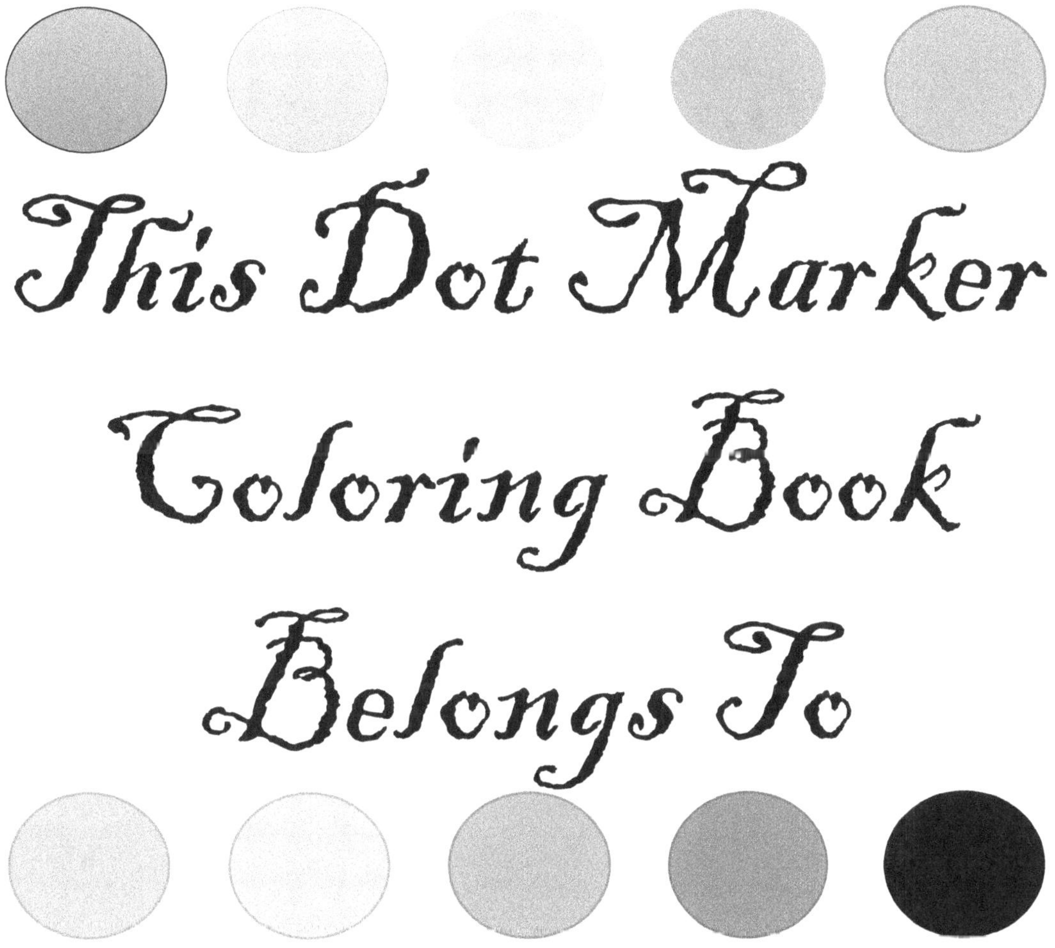

This Dot Marker

Coloring Book

Belongs To

Please Don't
Forget to
Rate This
Book

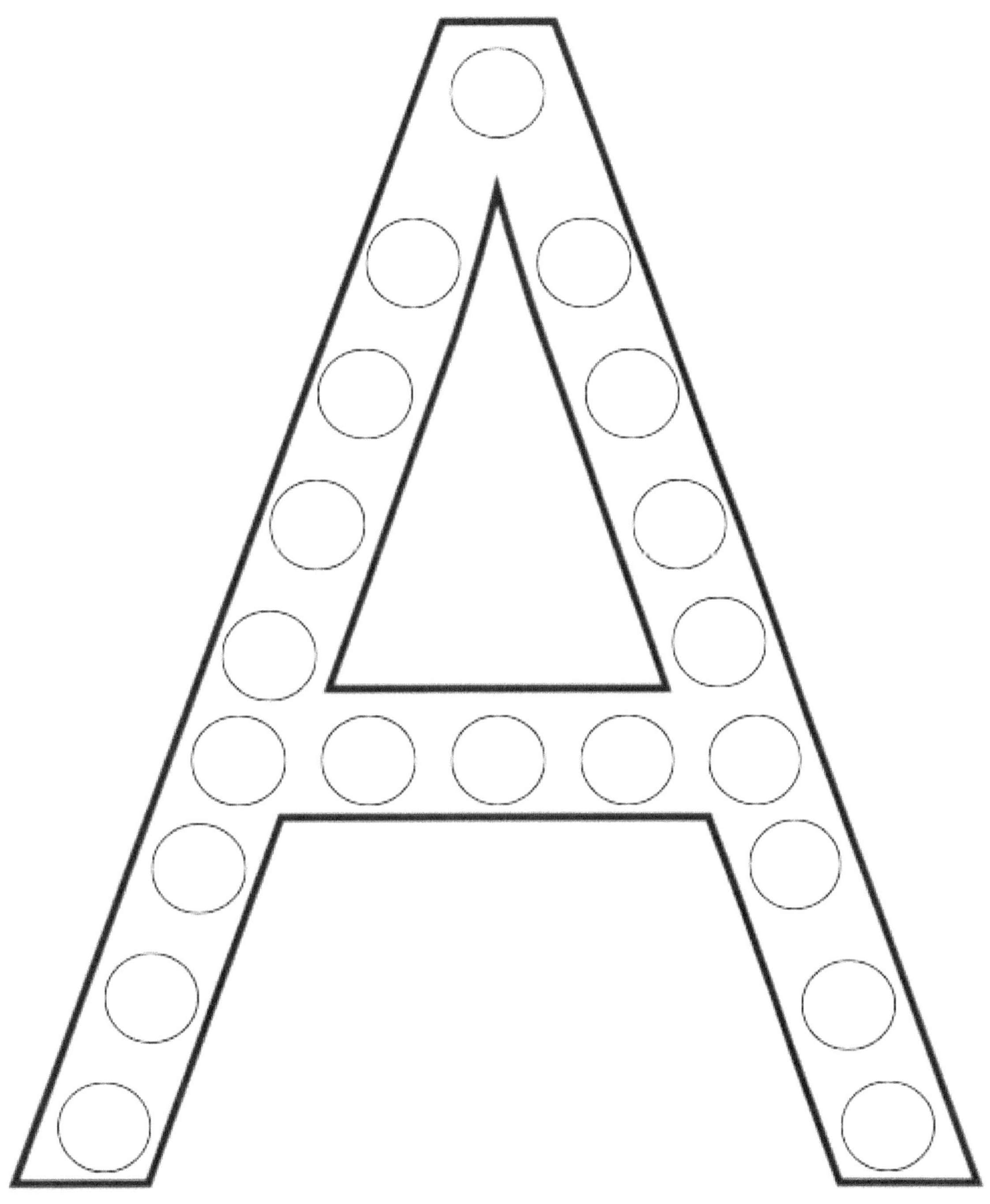

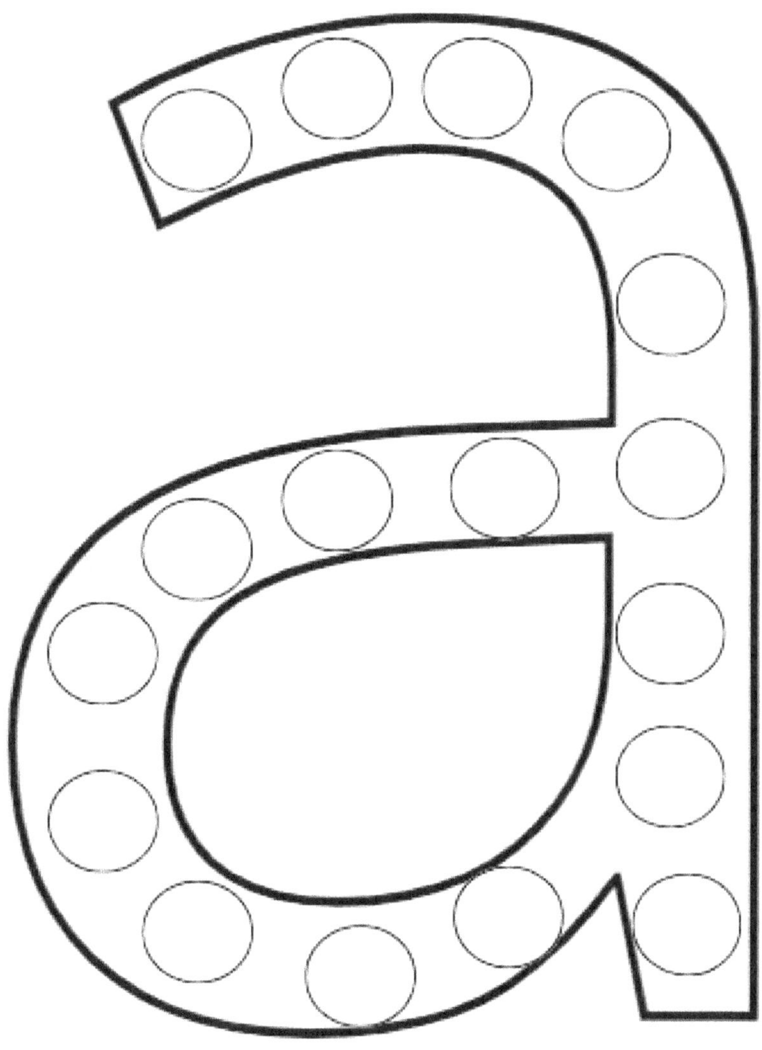

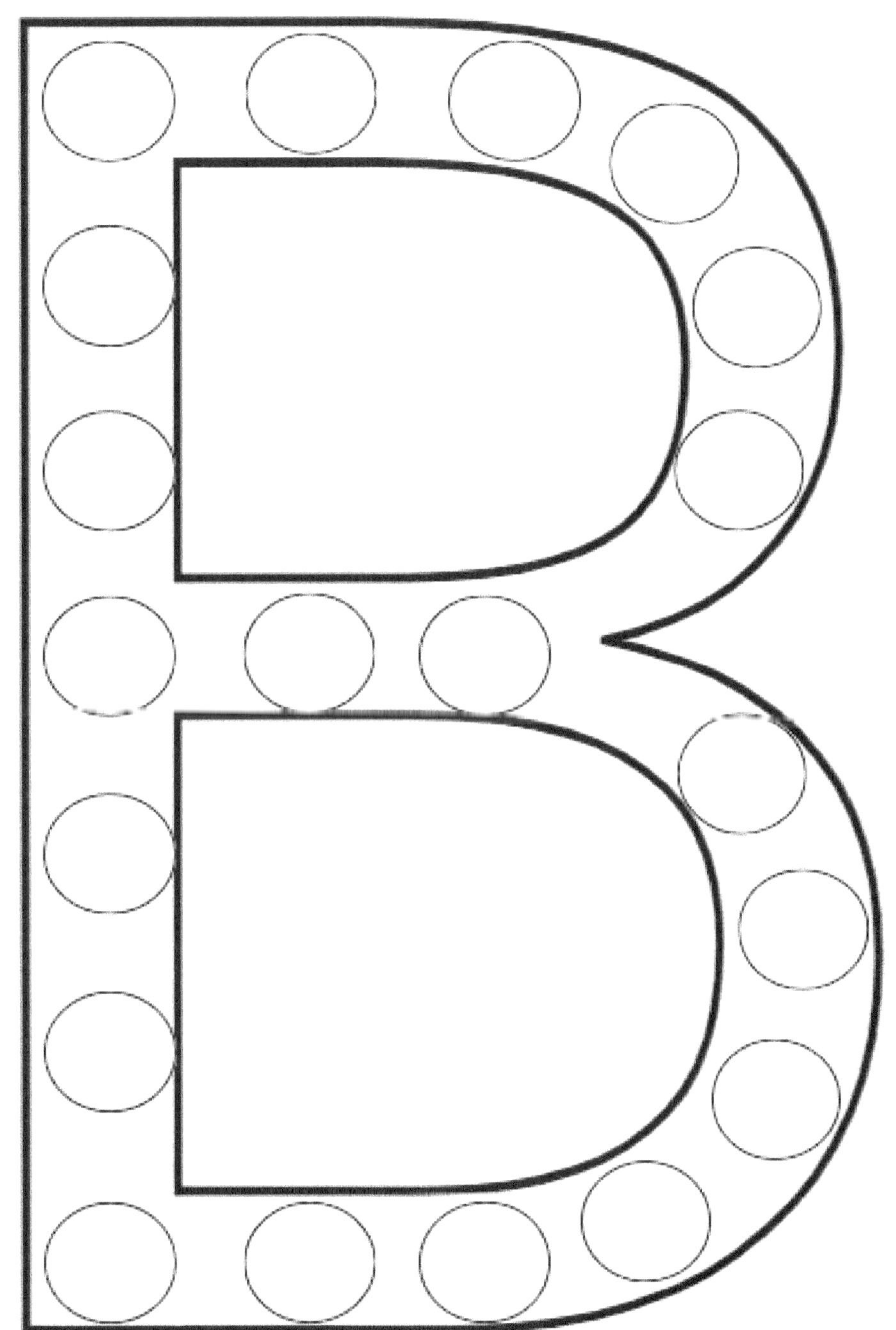

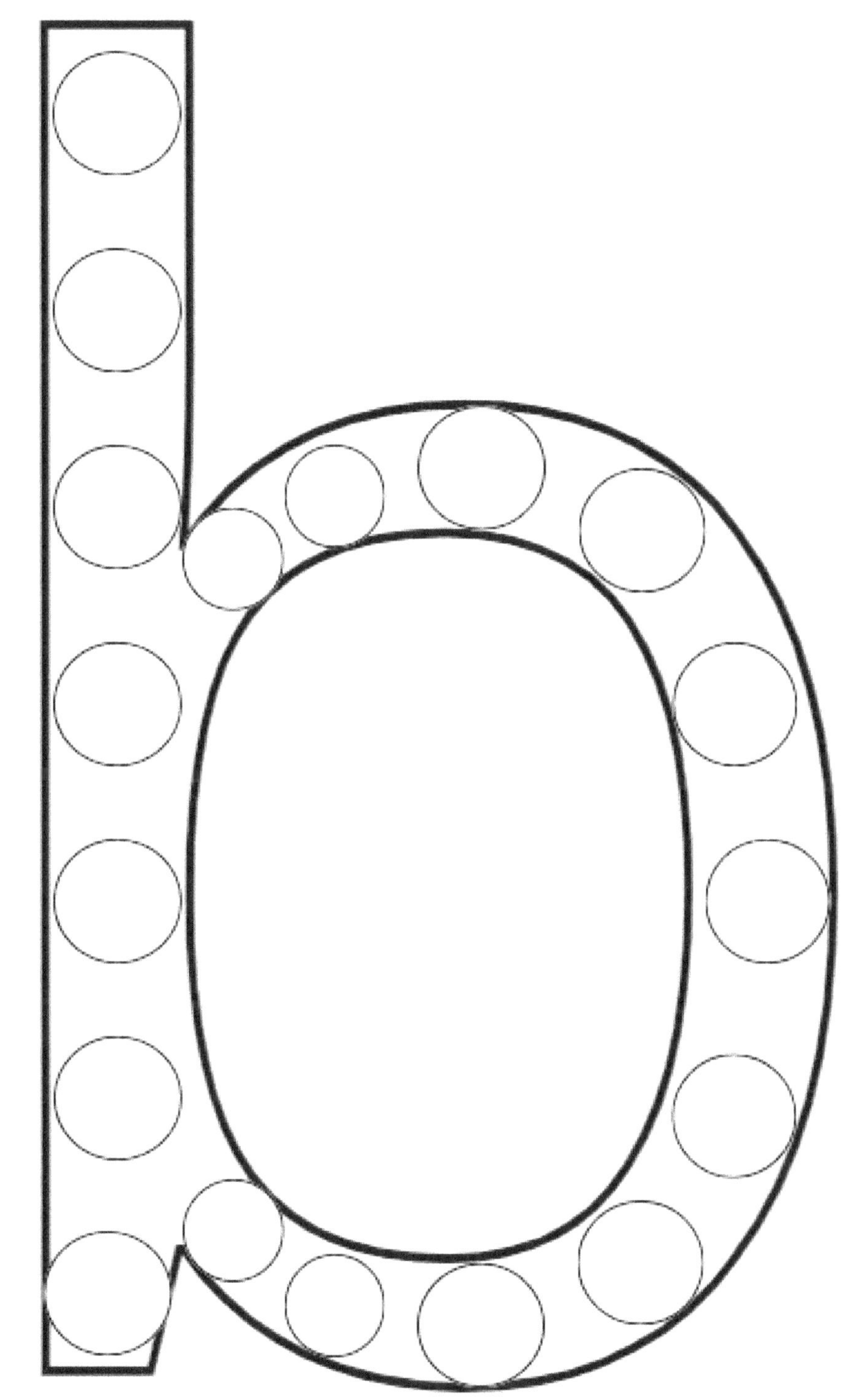

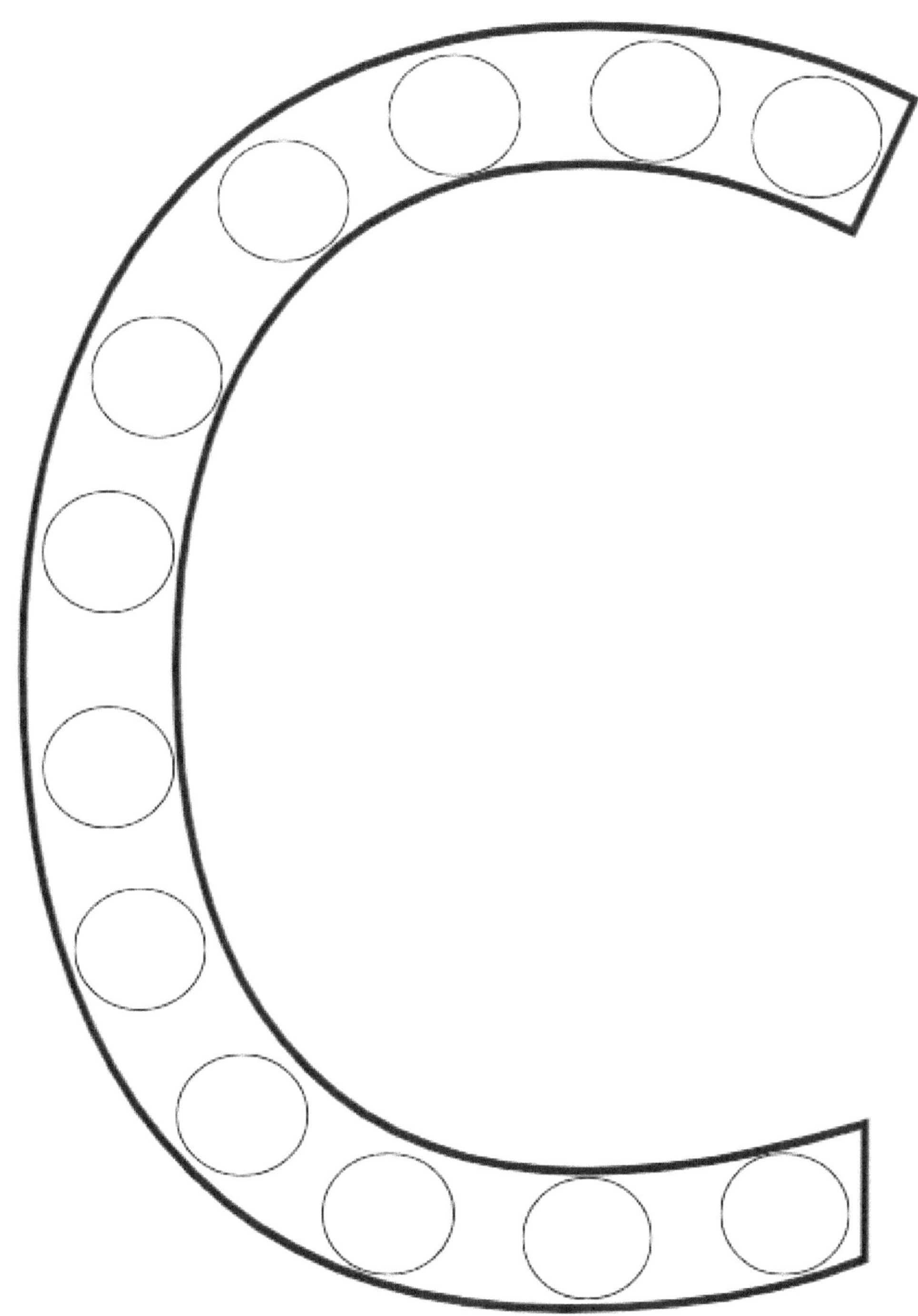

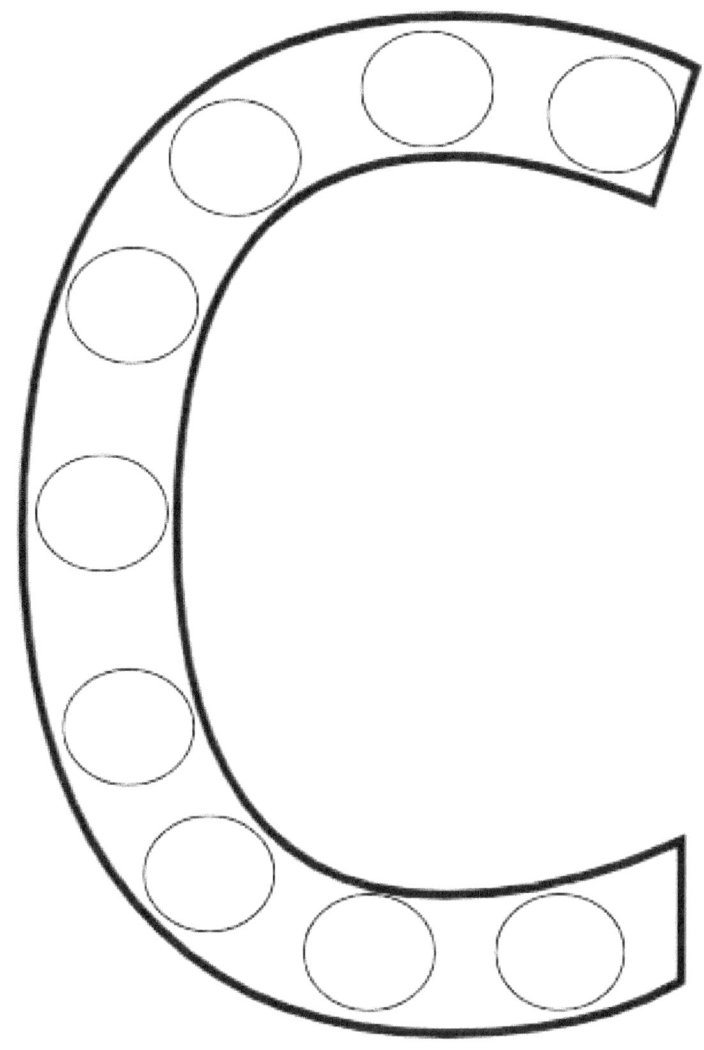

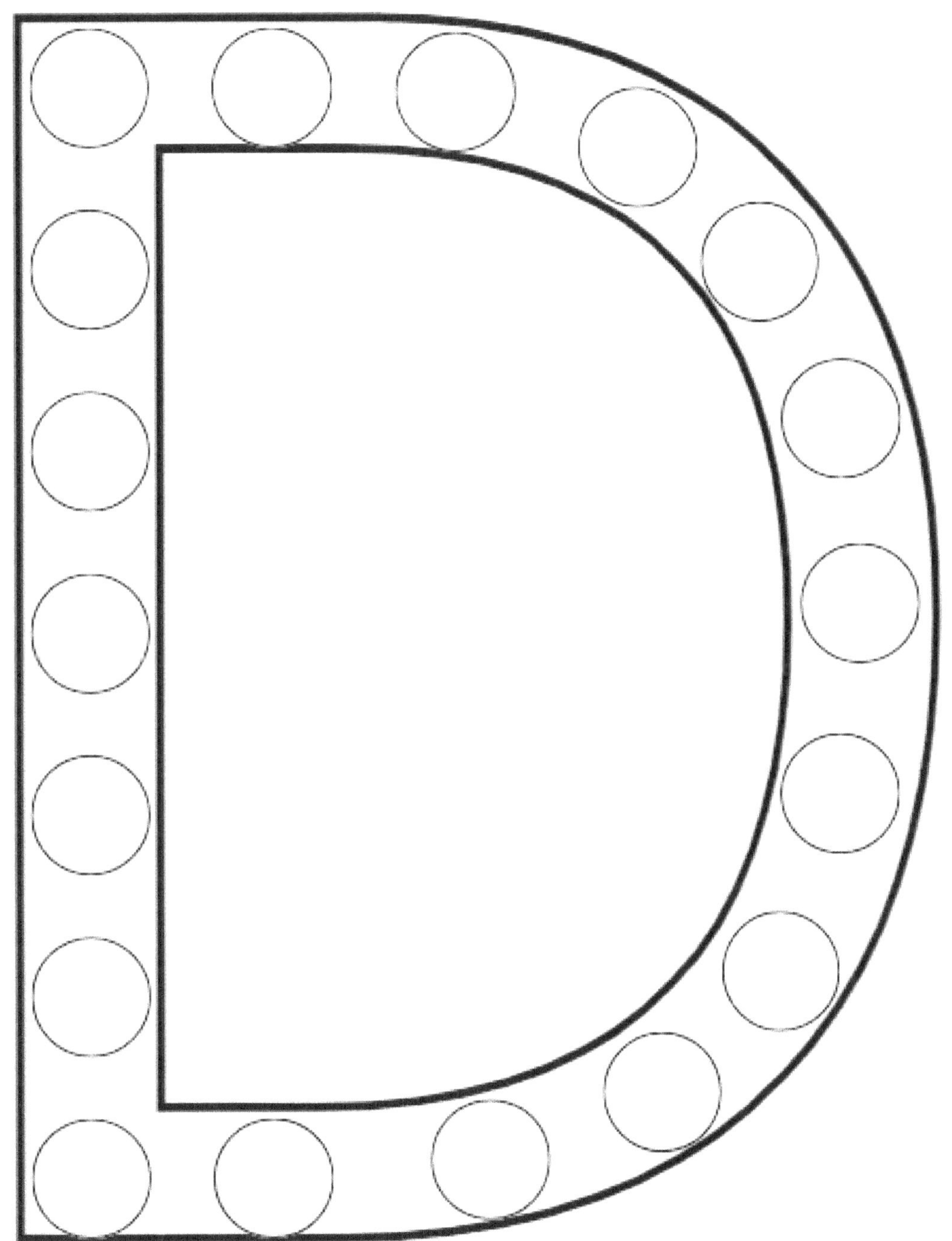

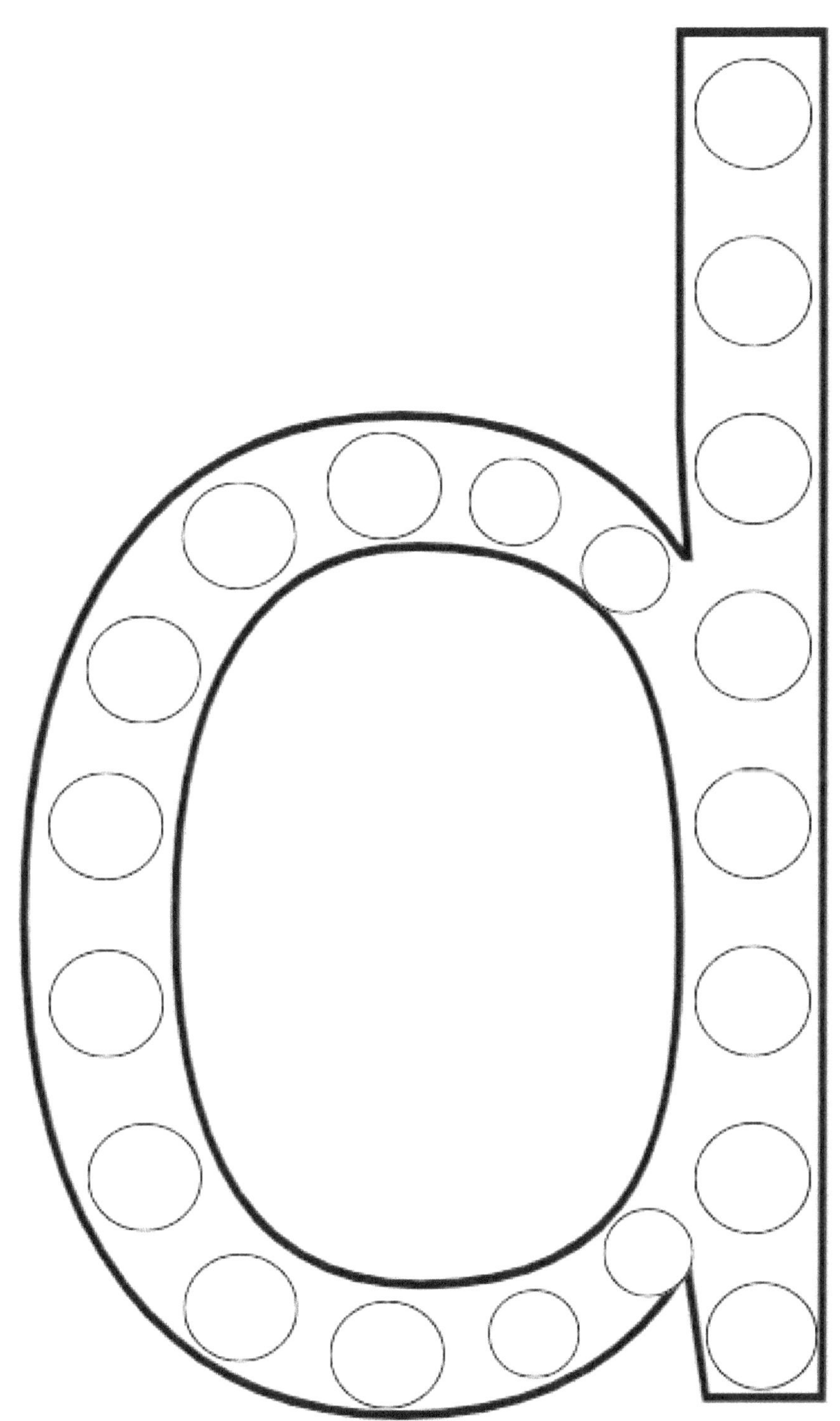

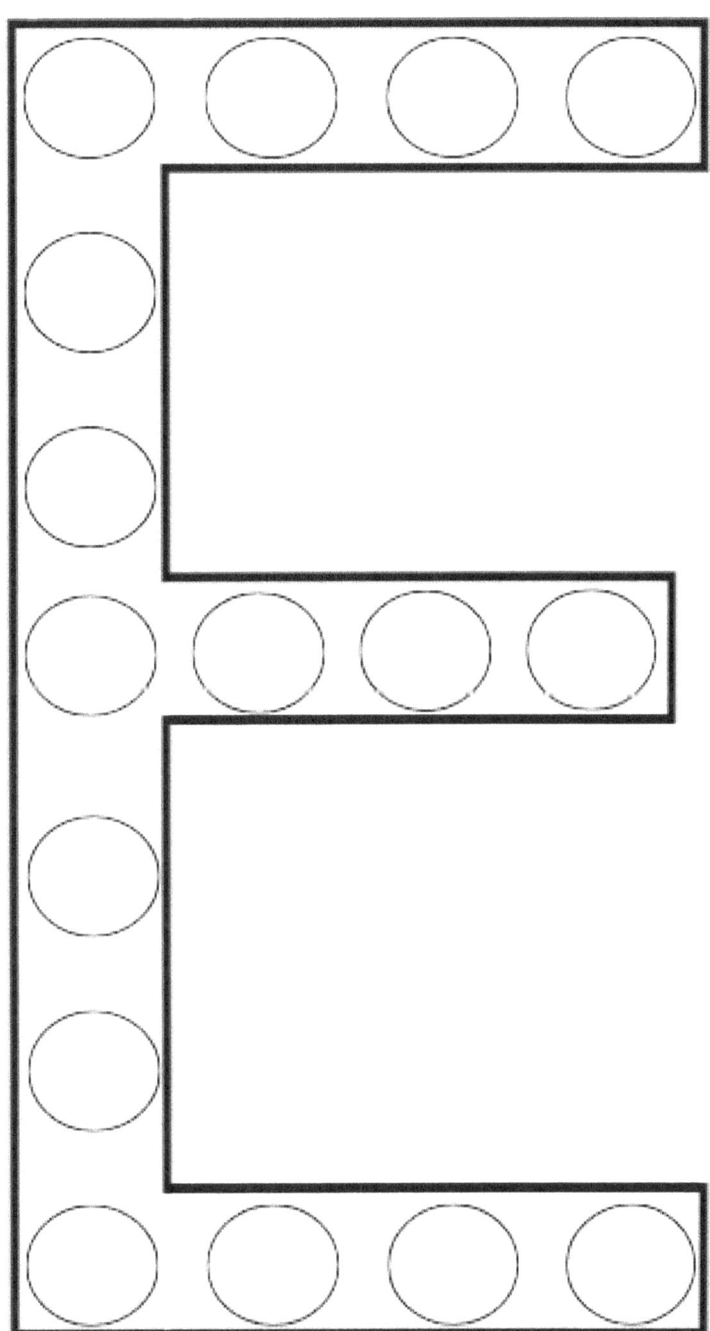

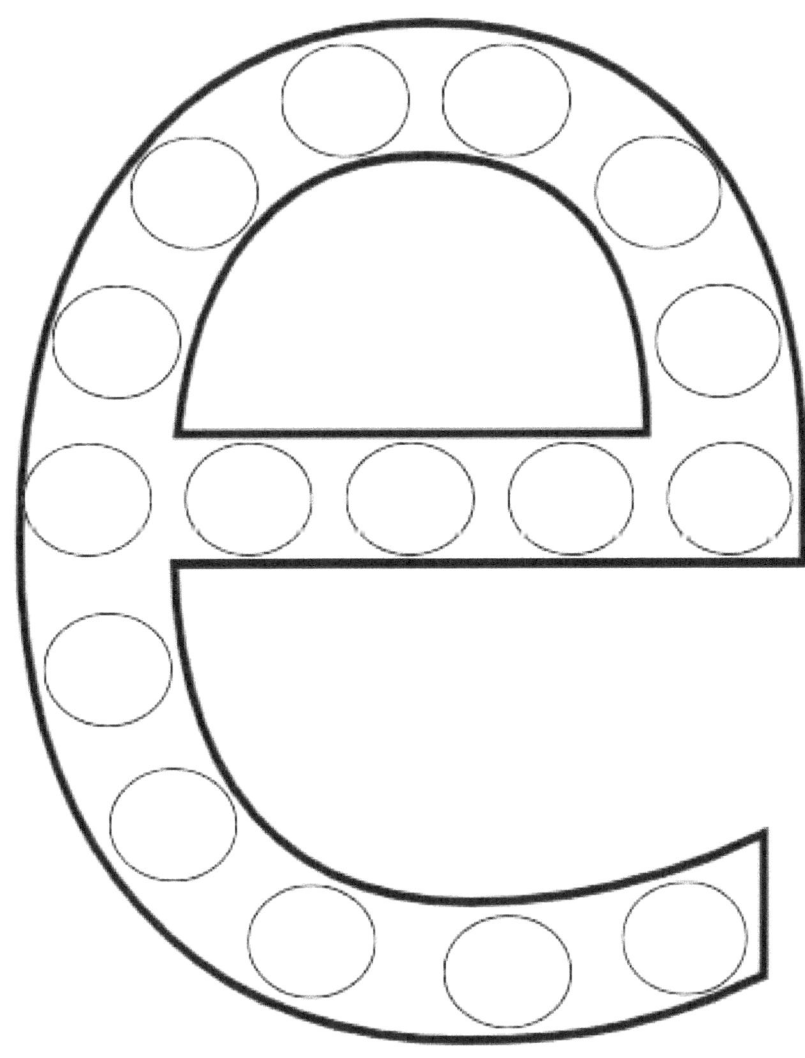

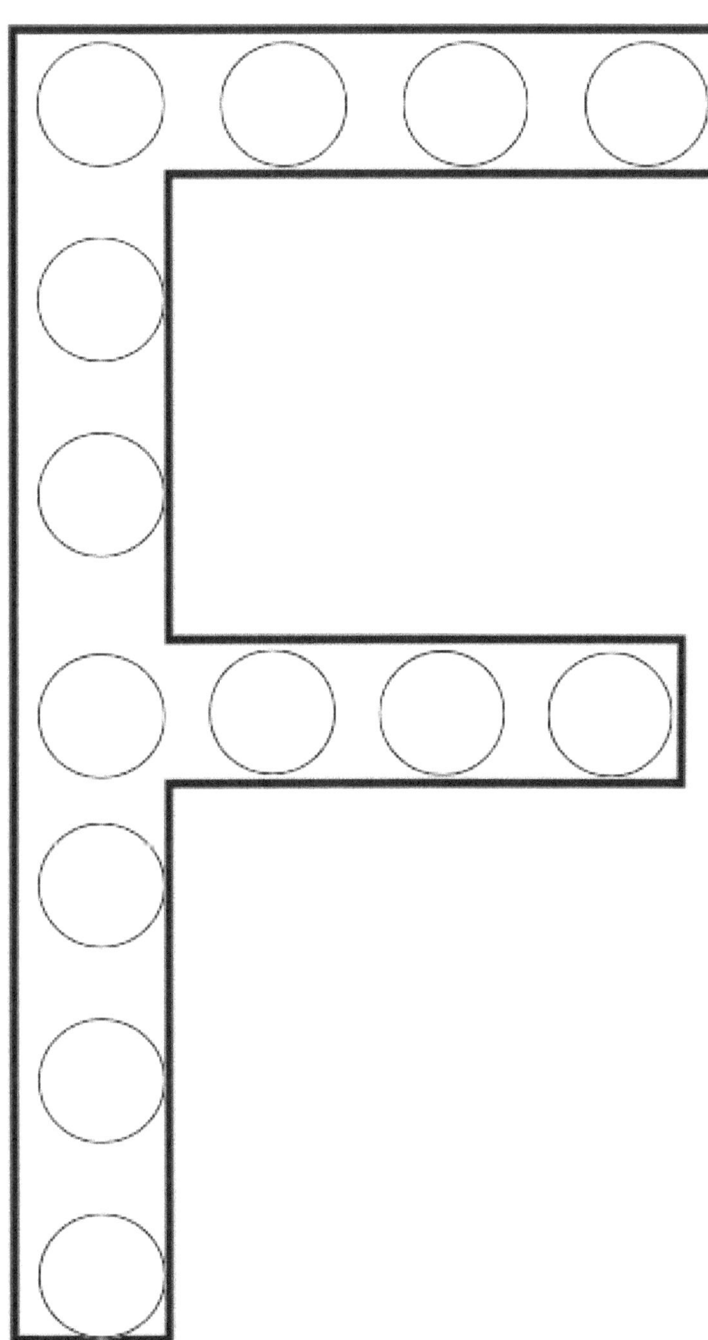

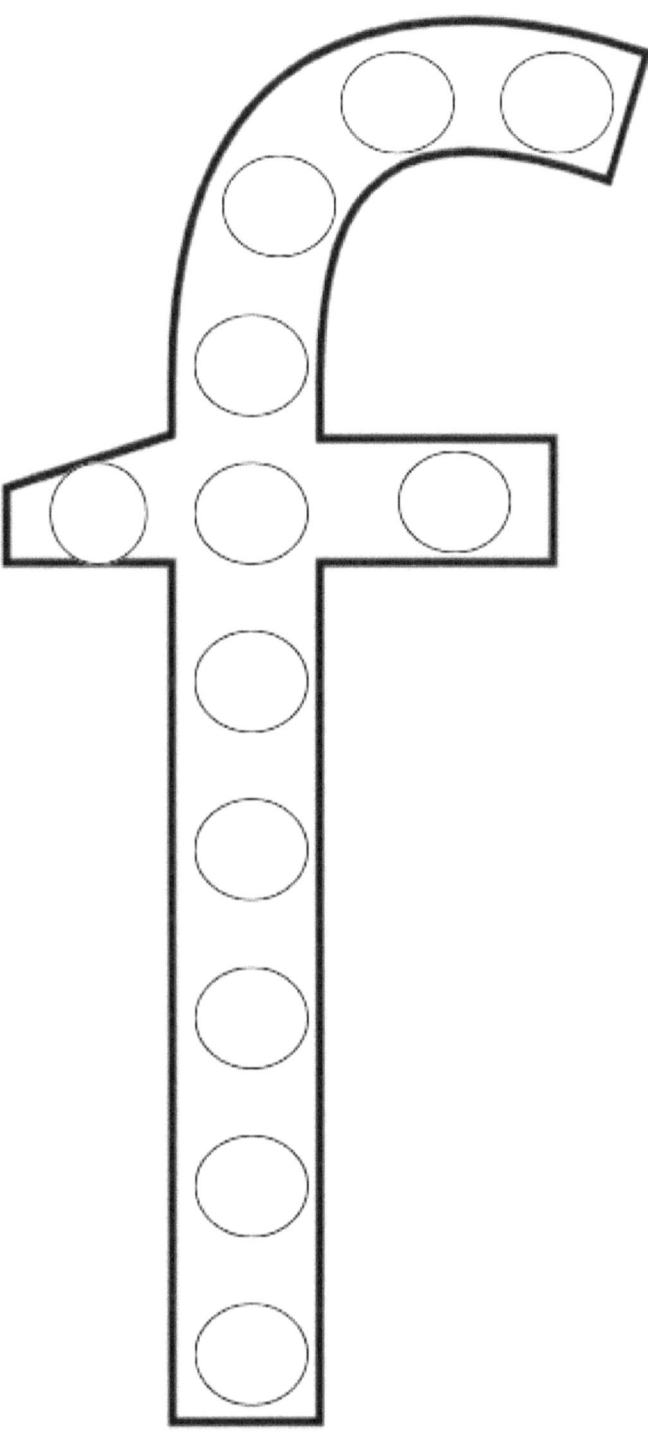

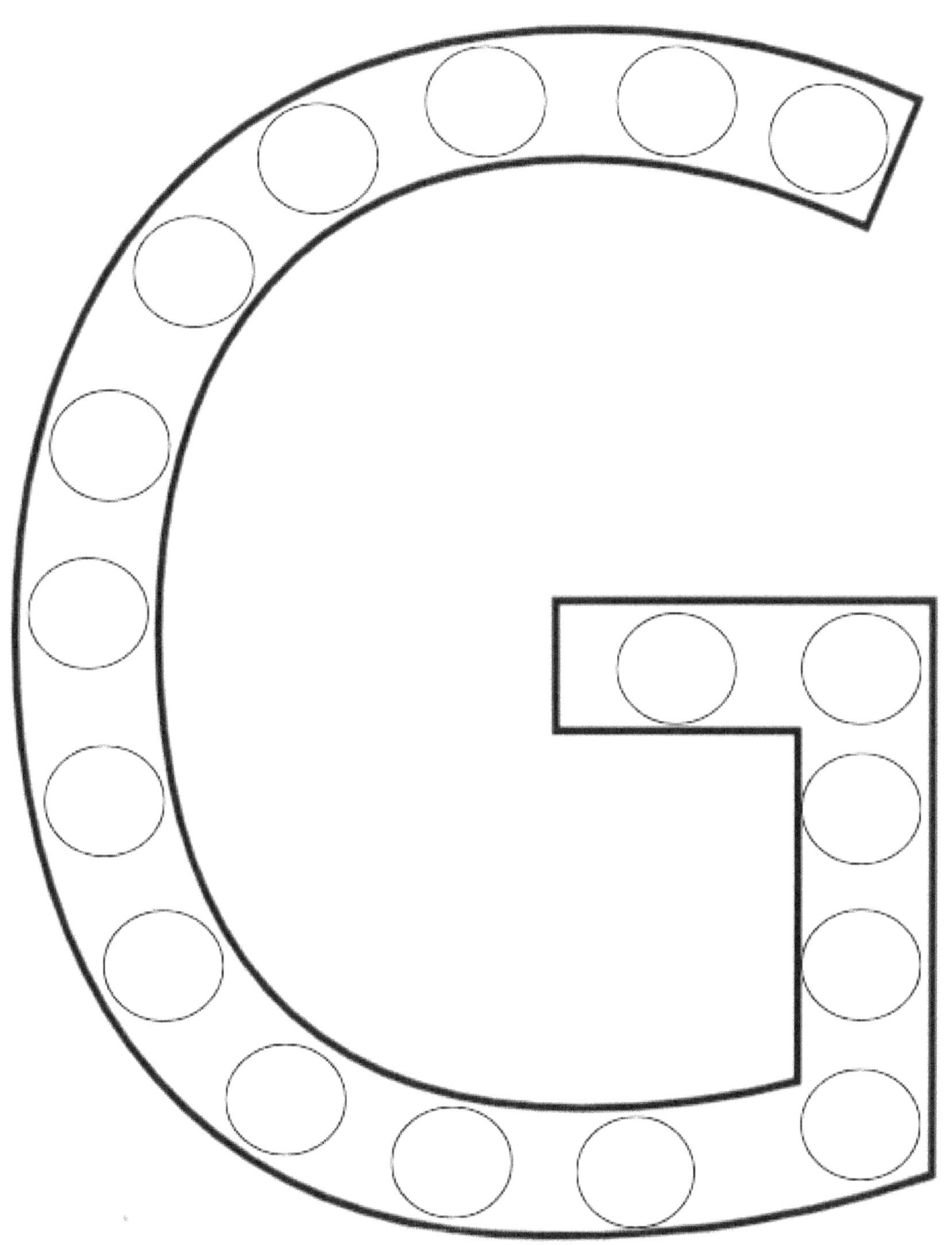

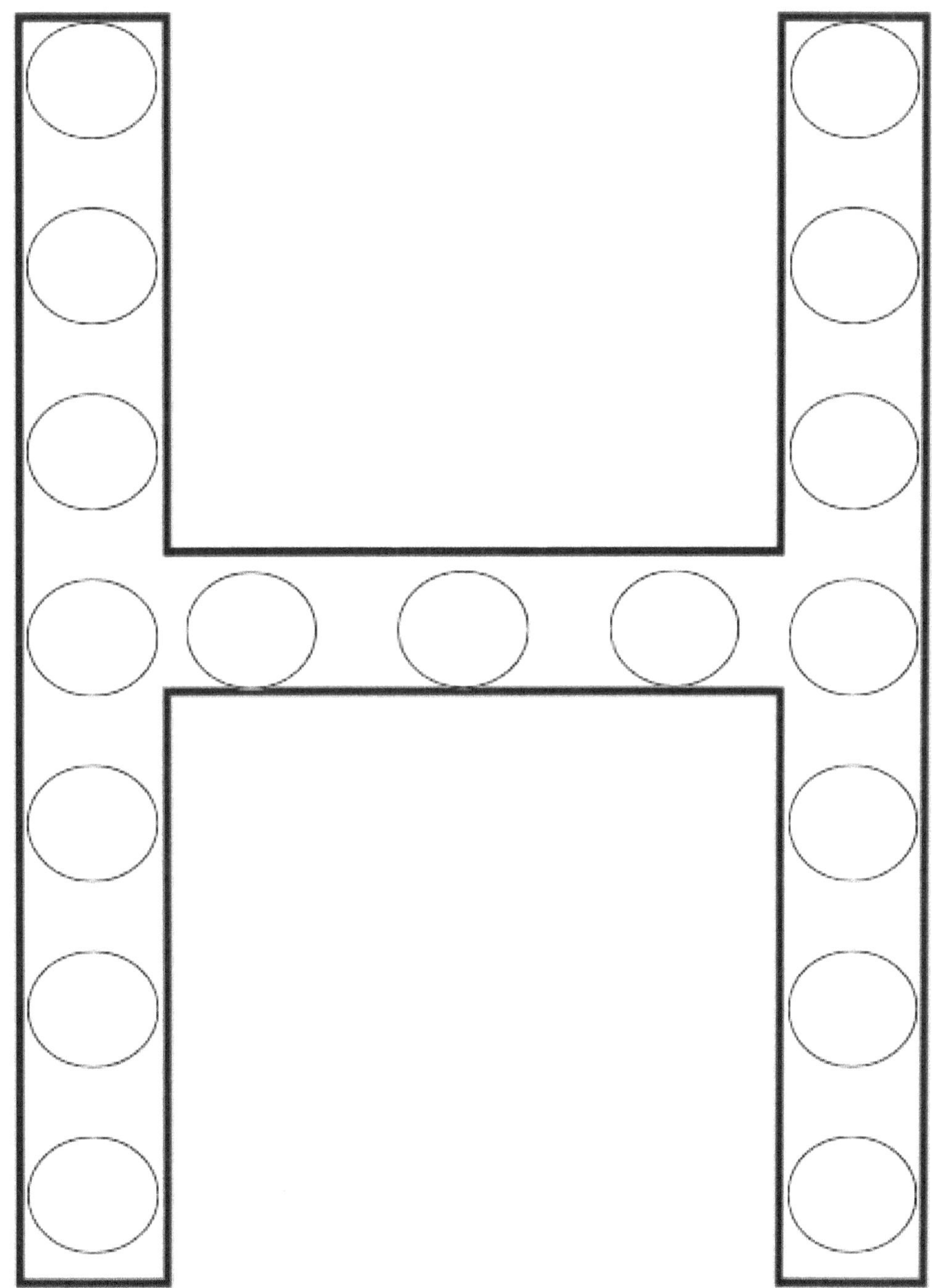

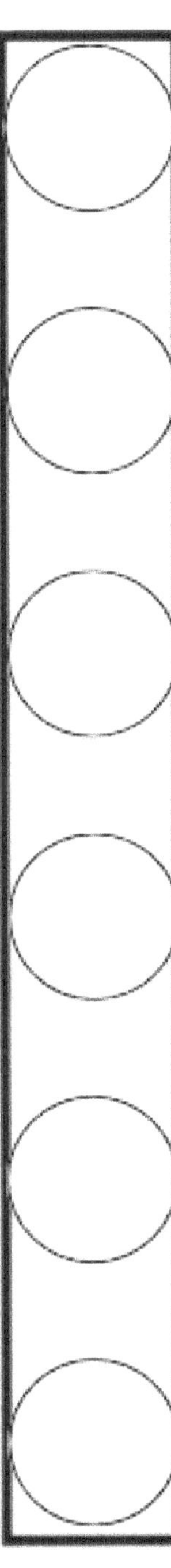

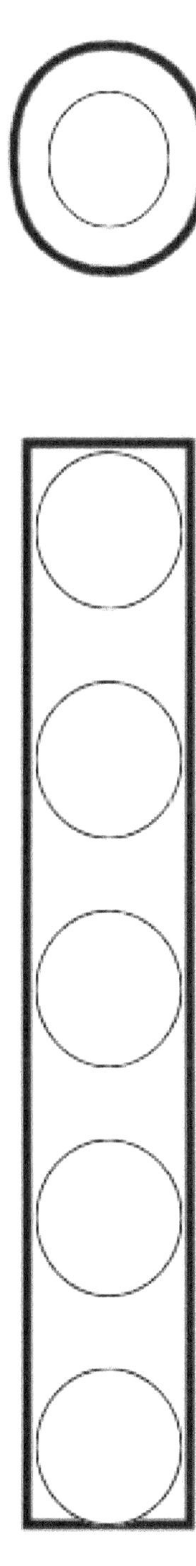

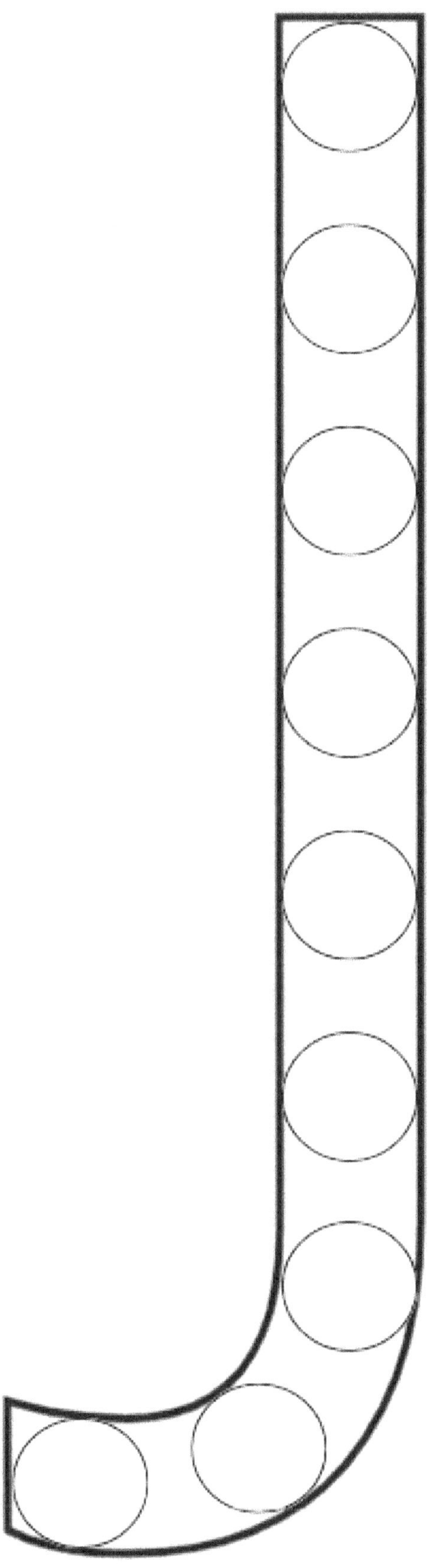

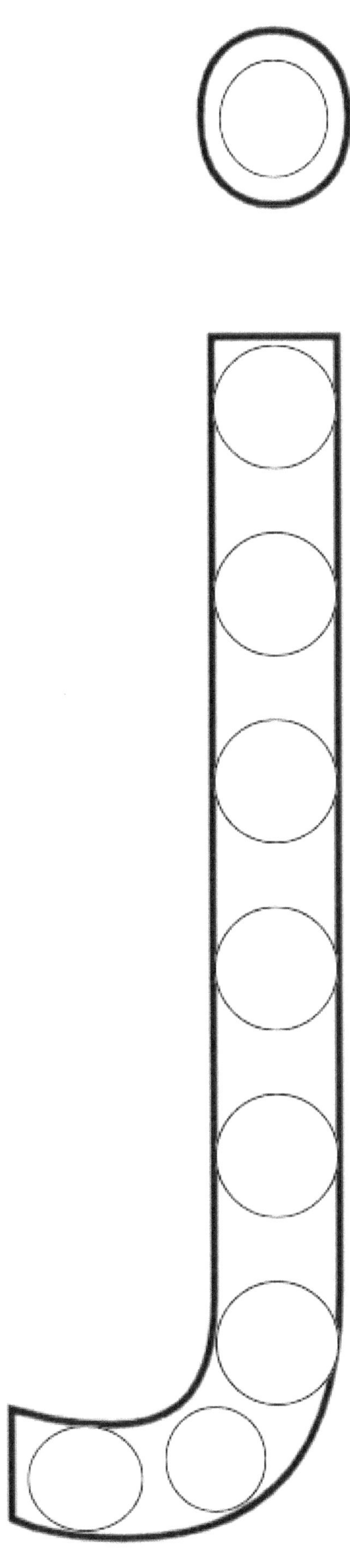

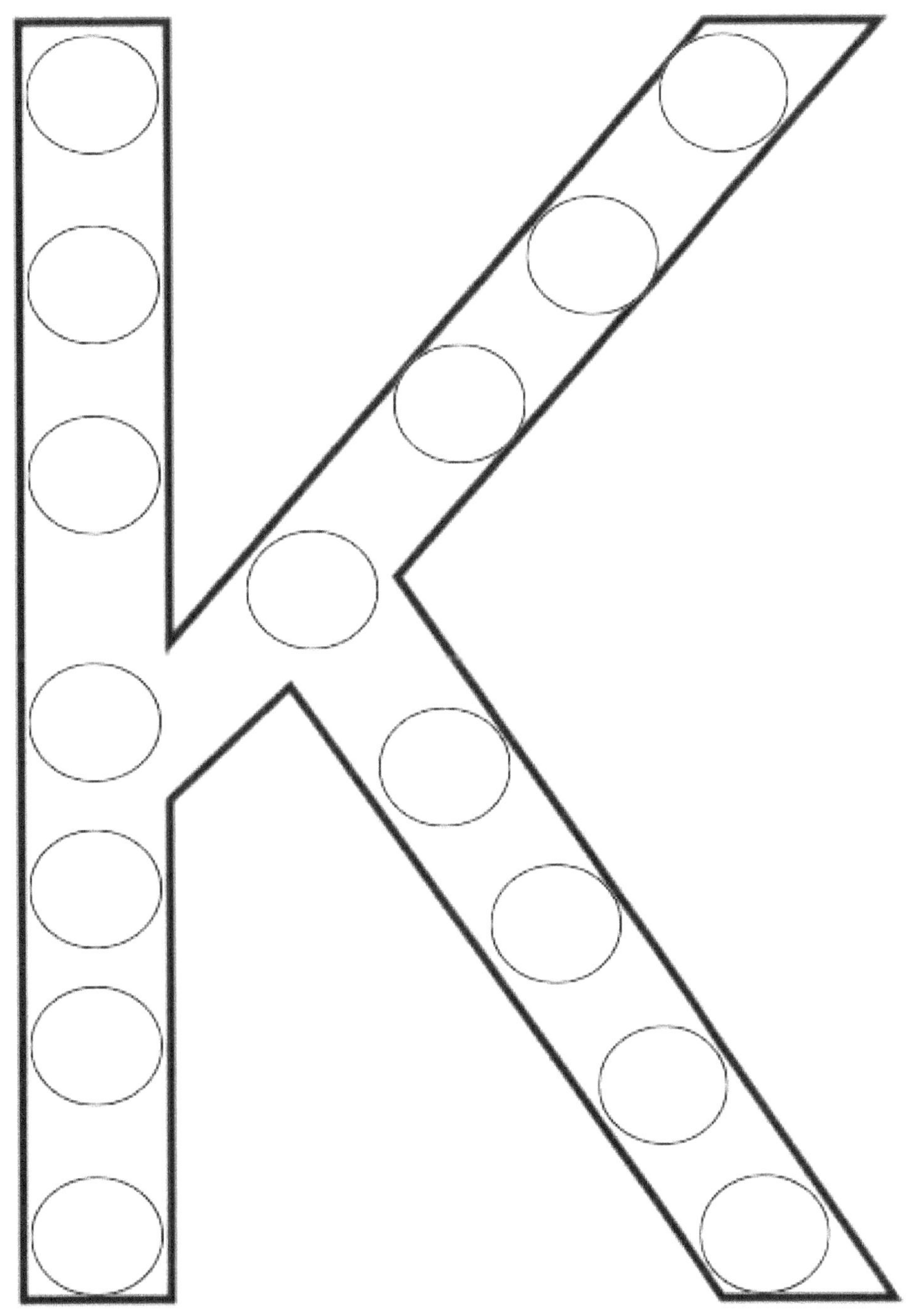

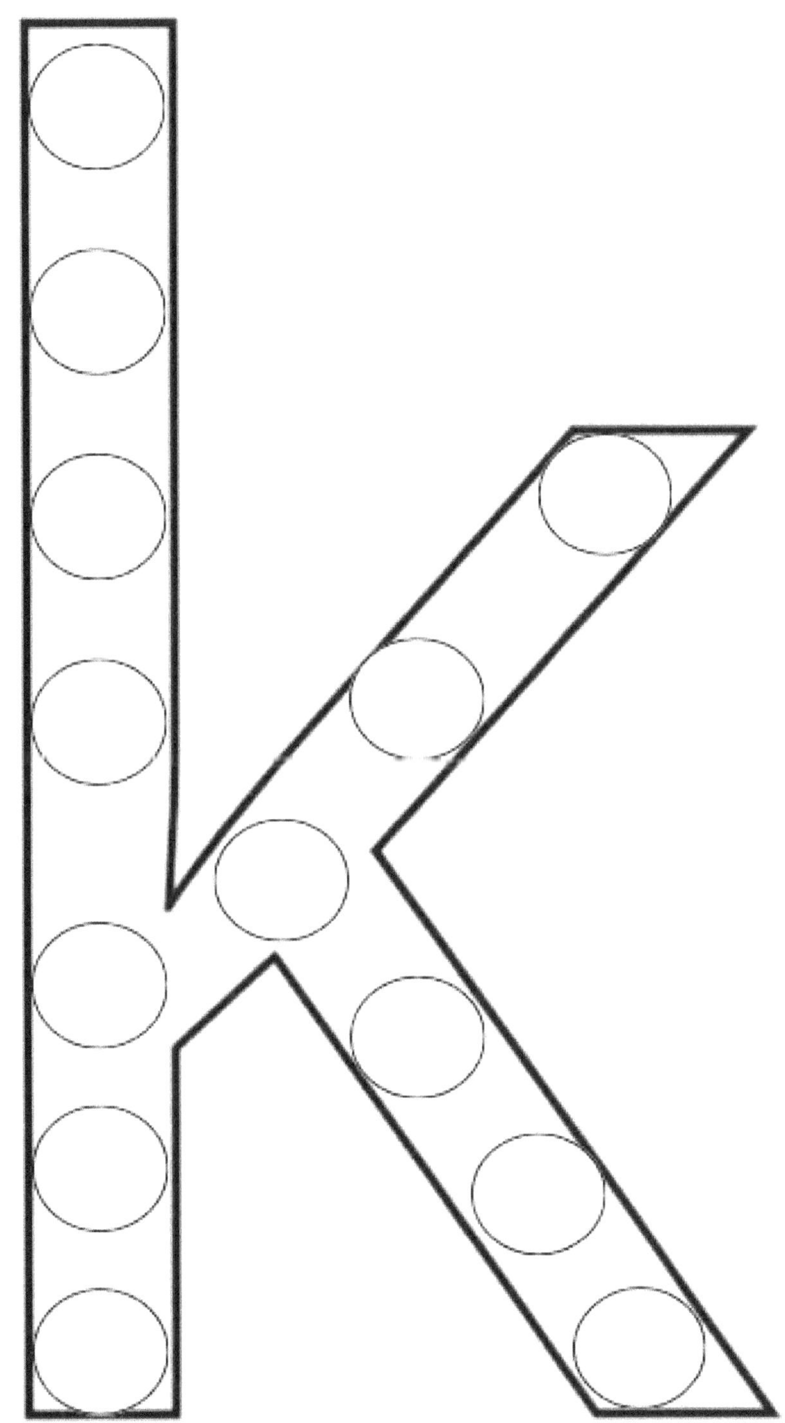

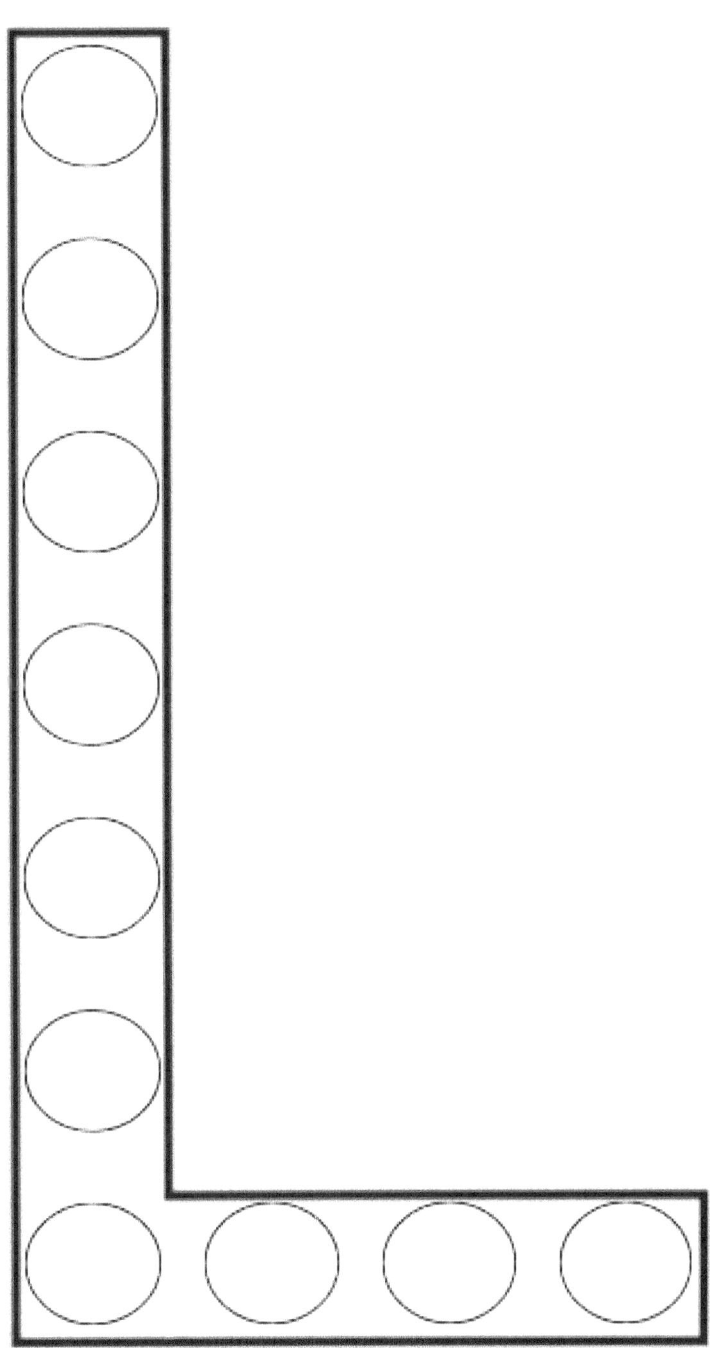

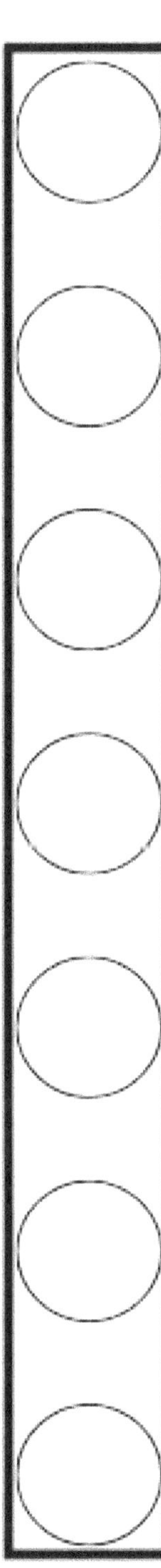

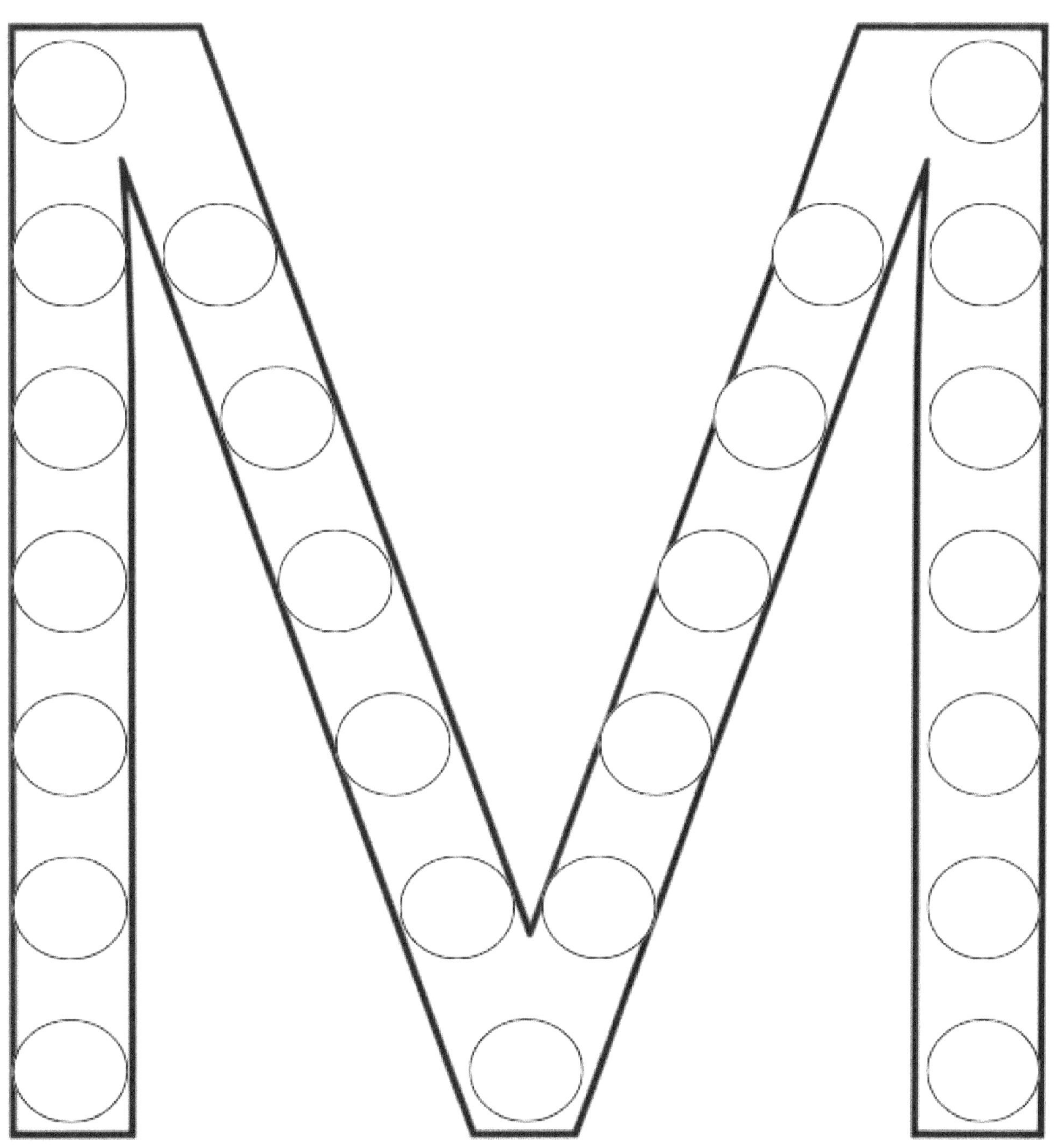

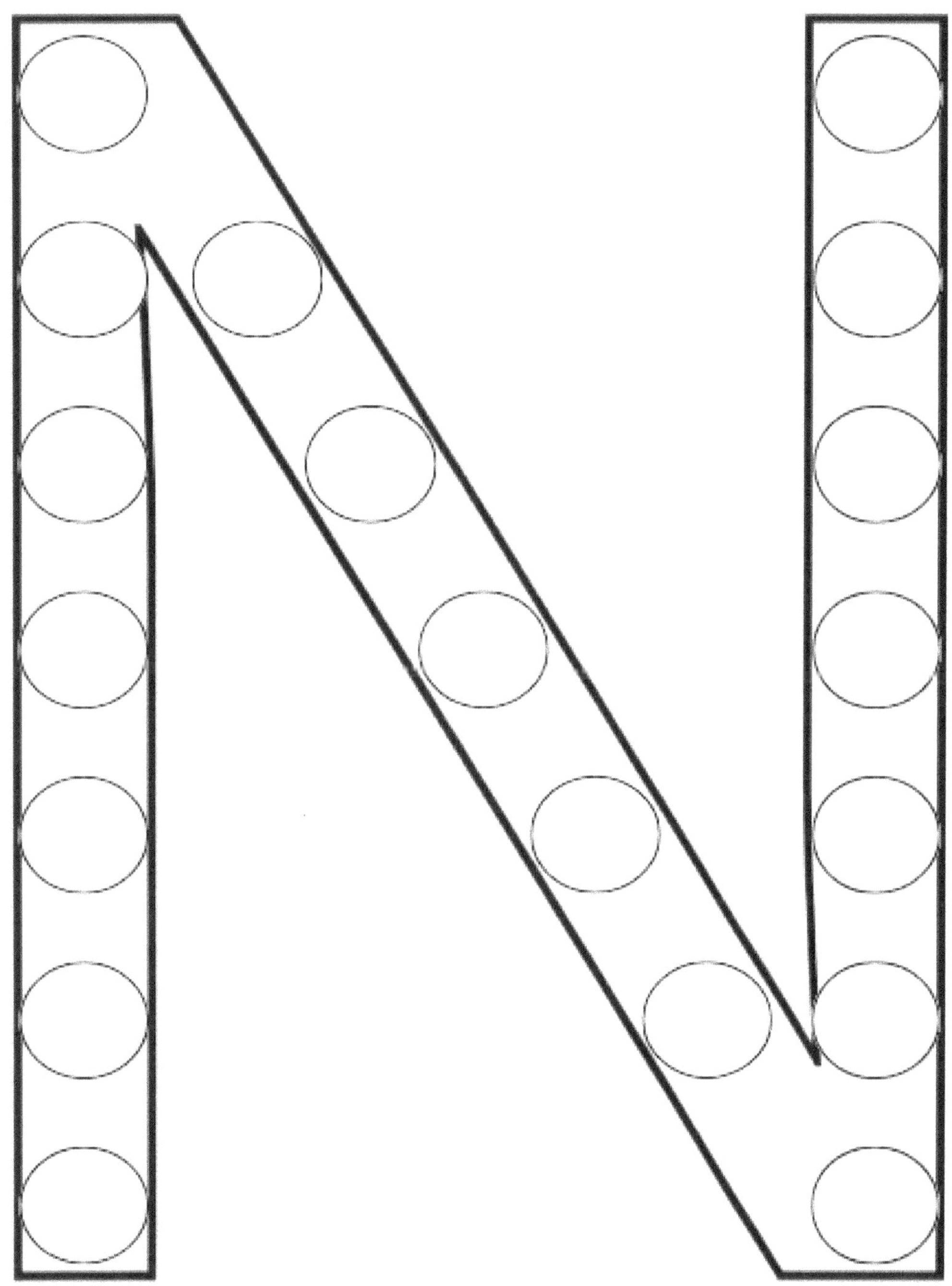

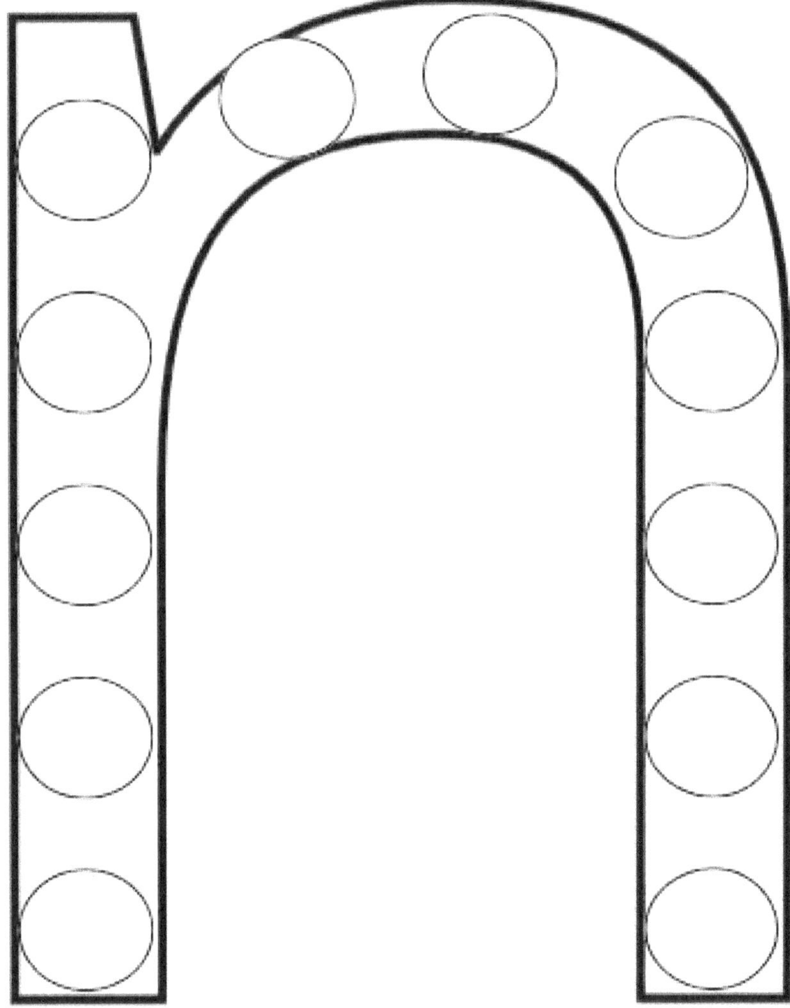

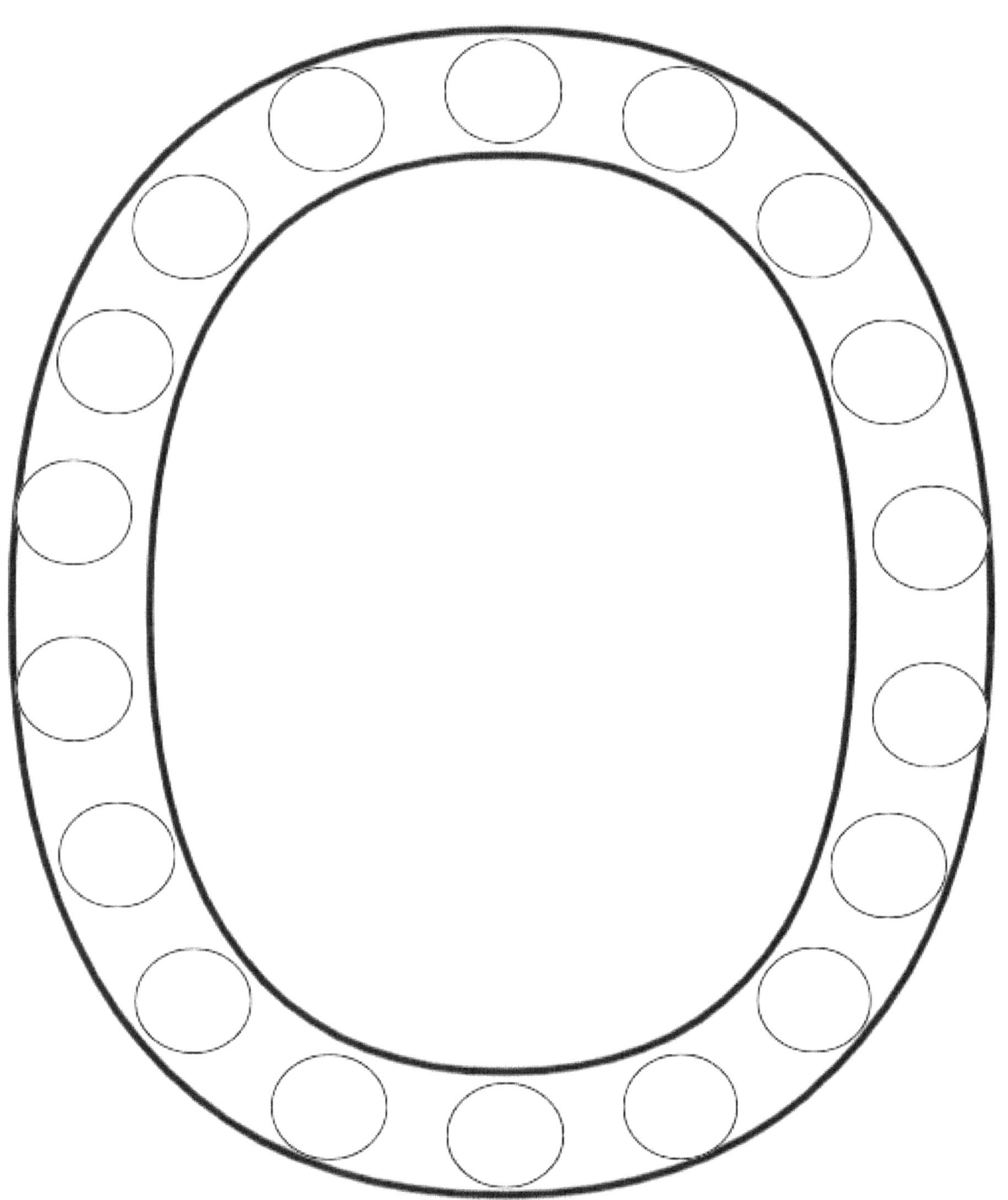

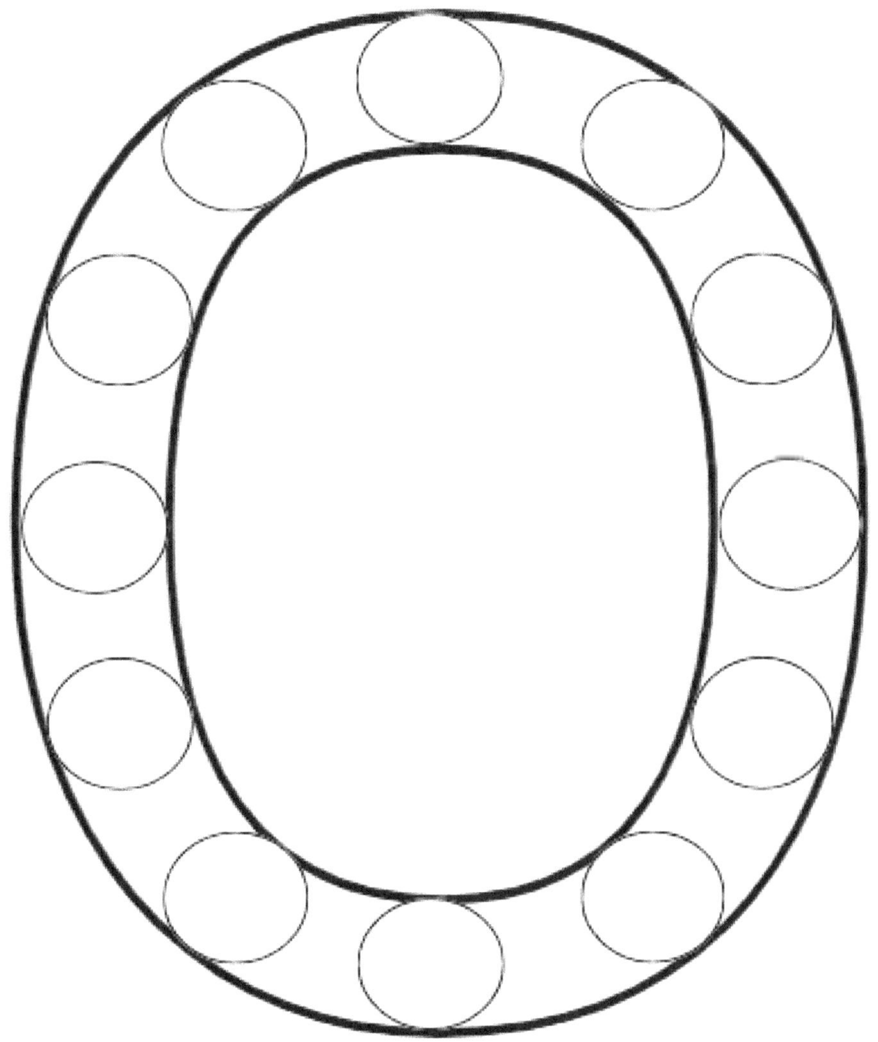

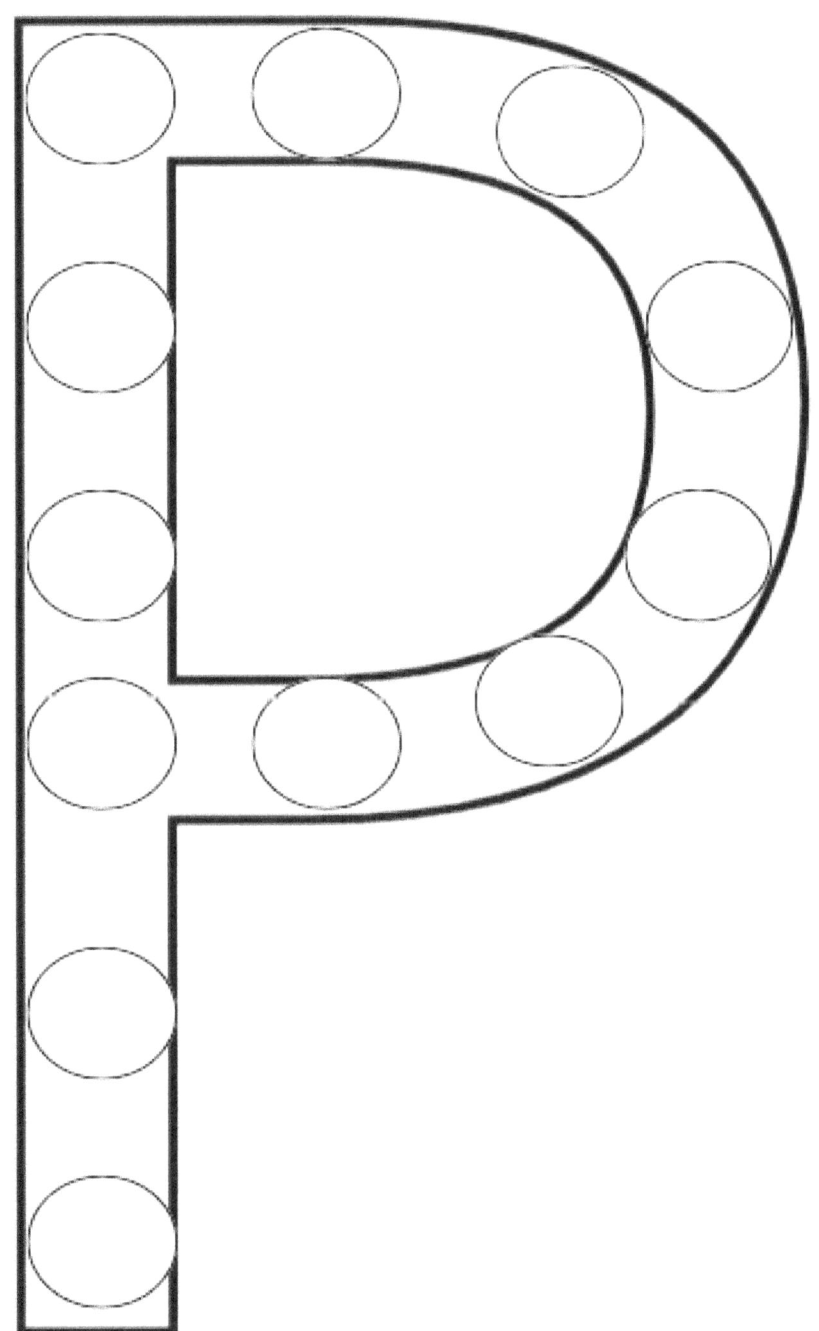

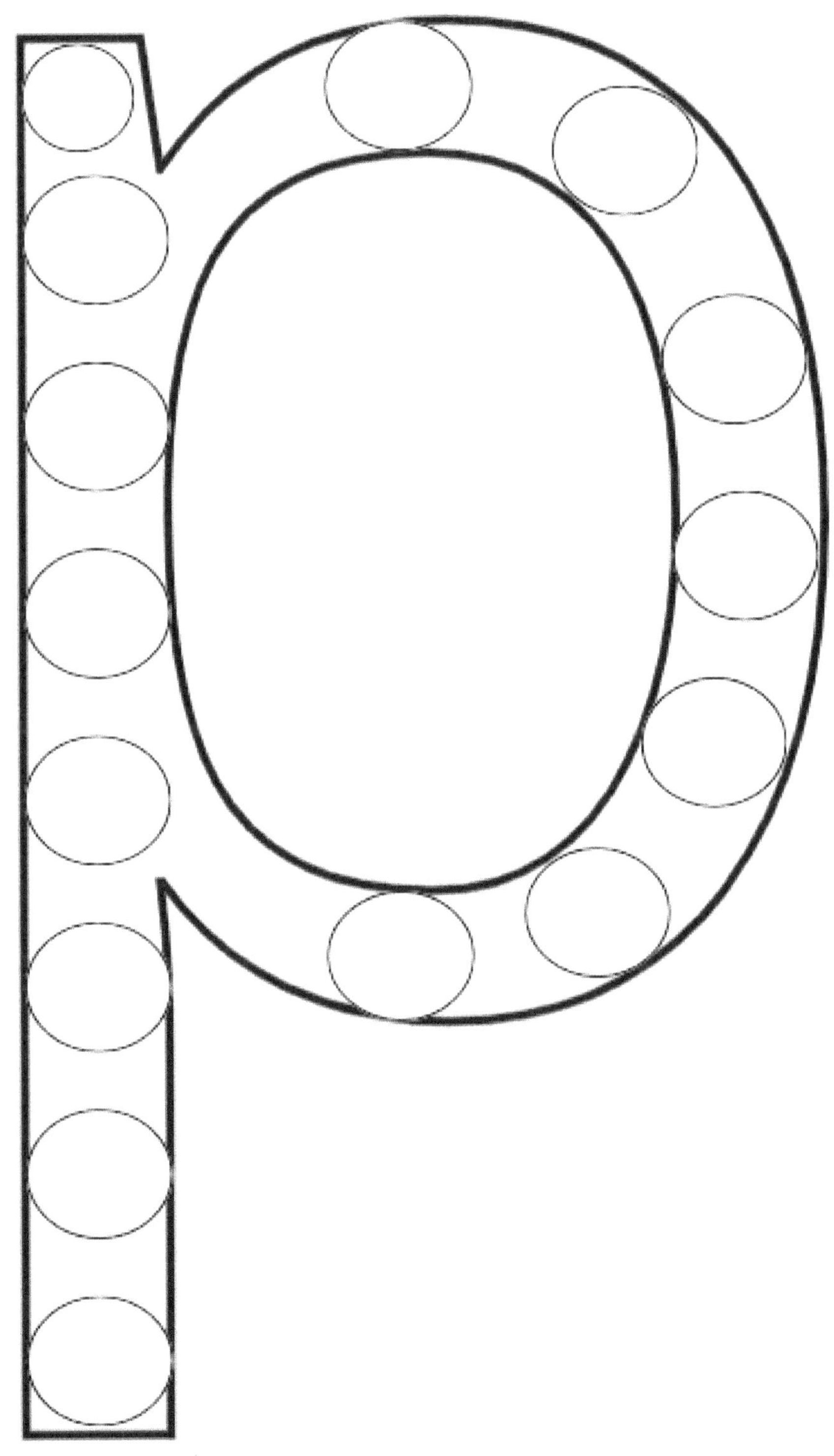

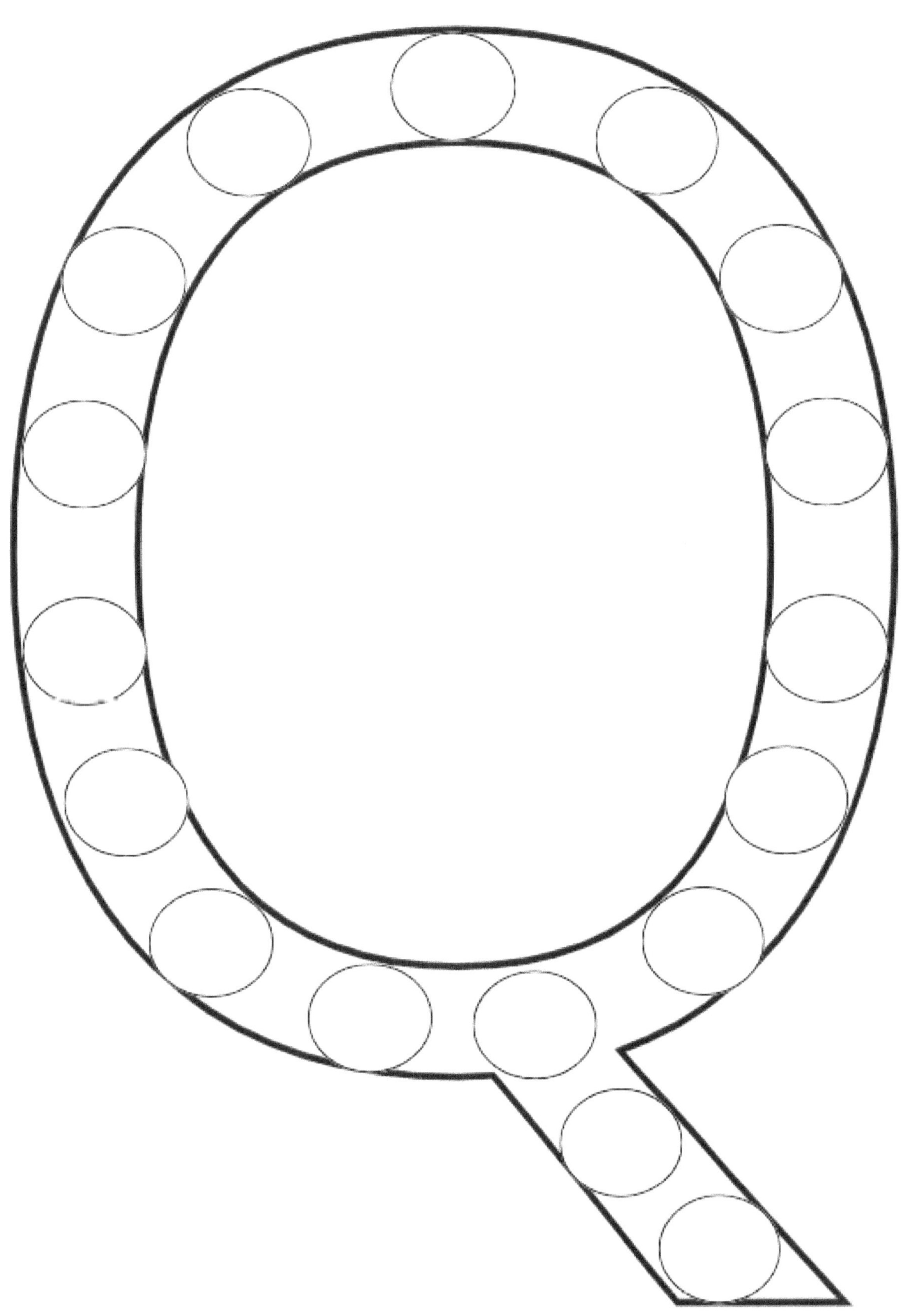

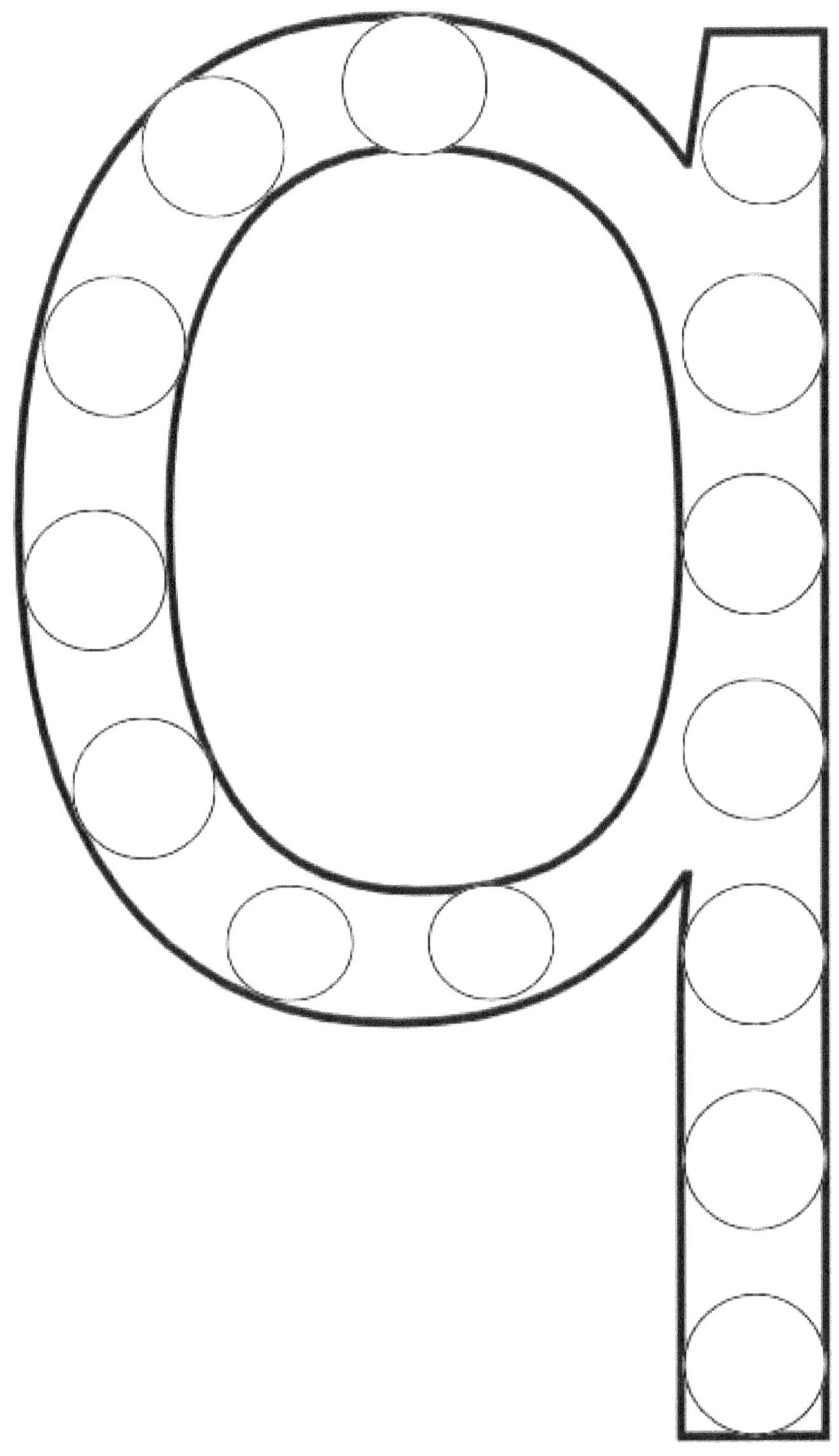

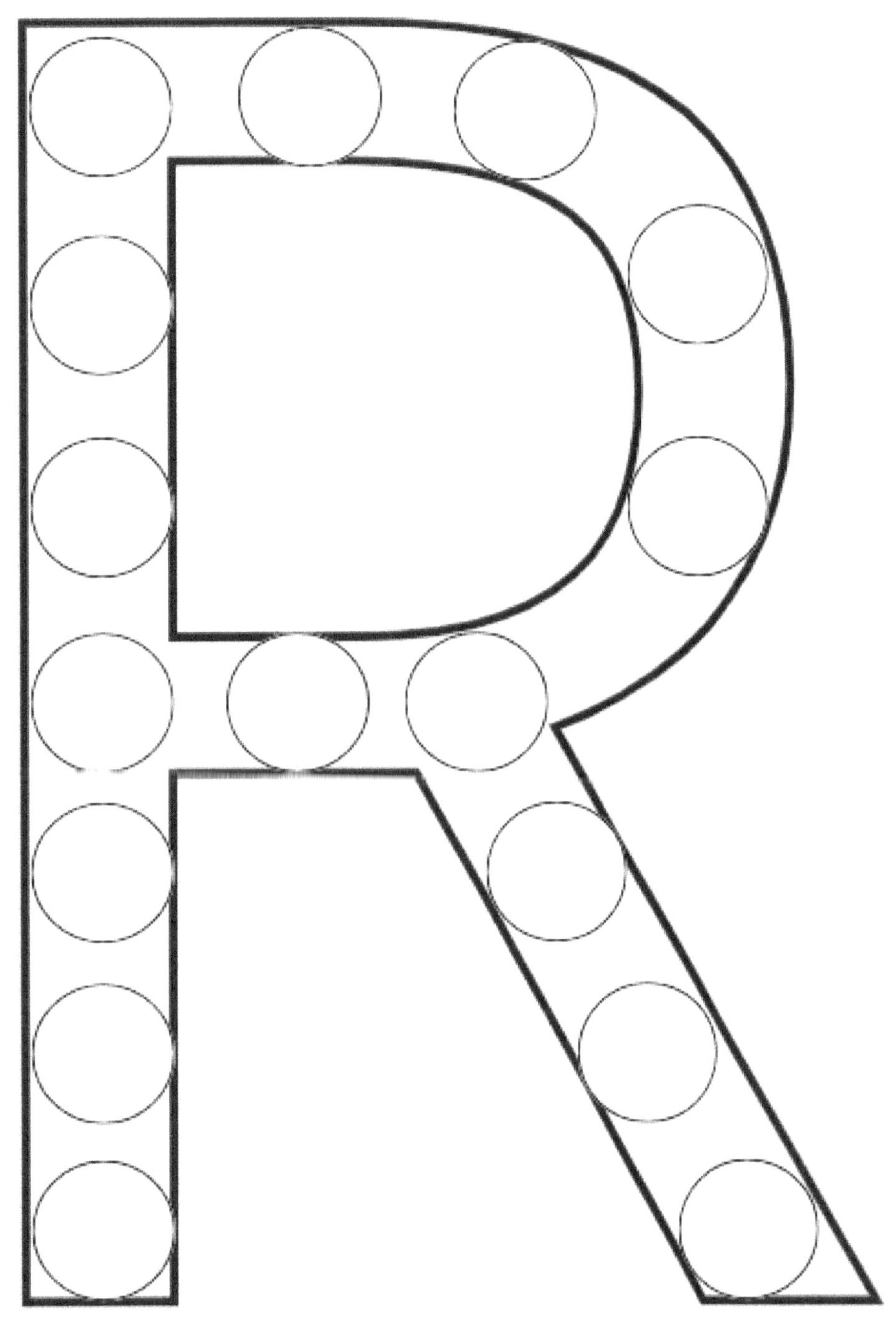

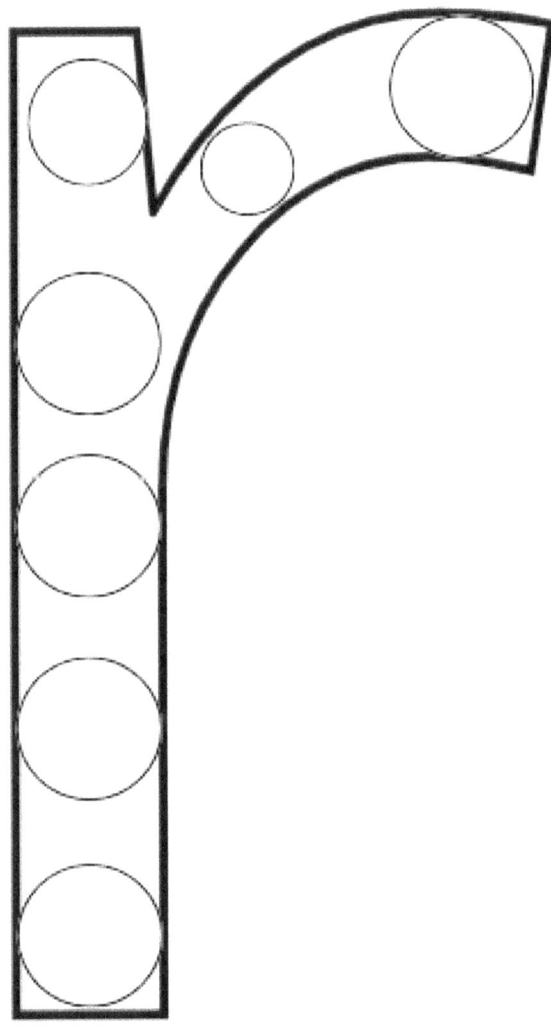

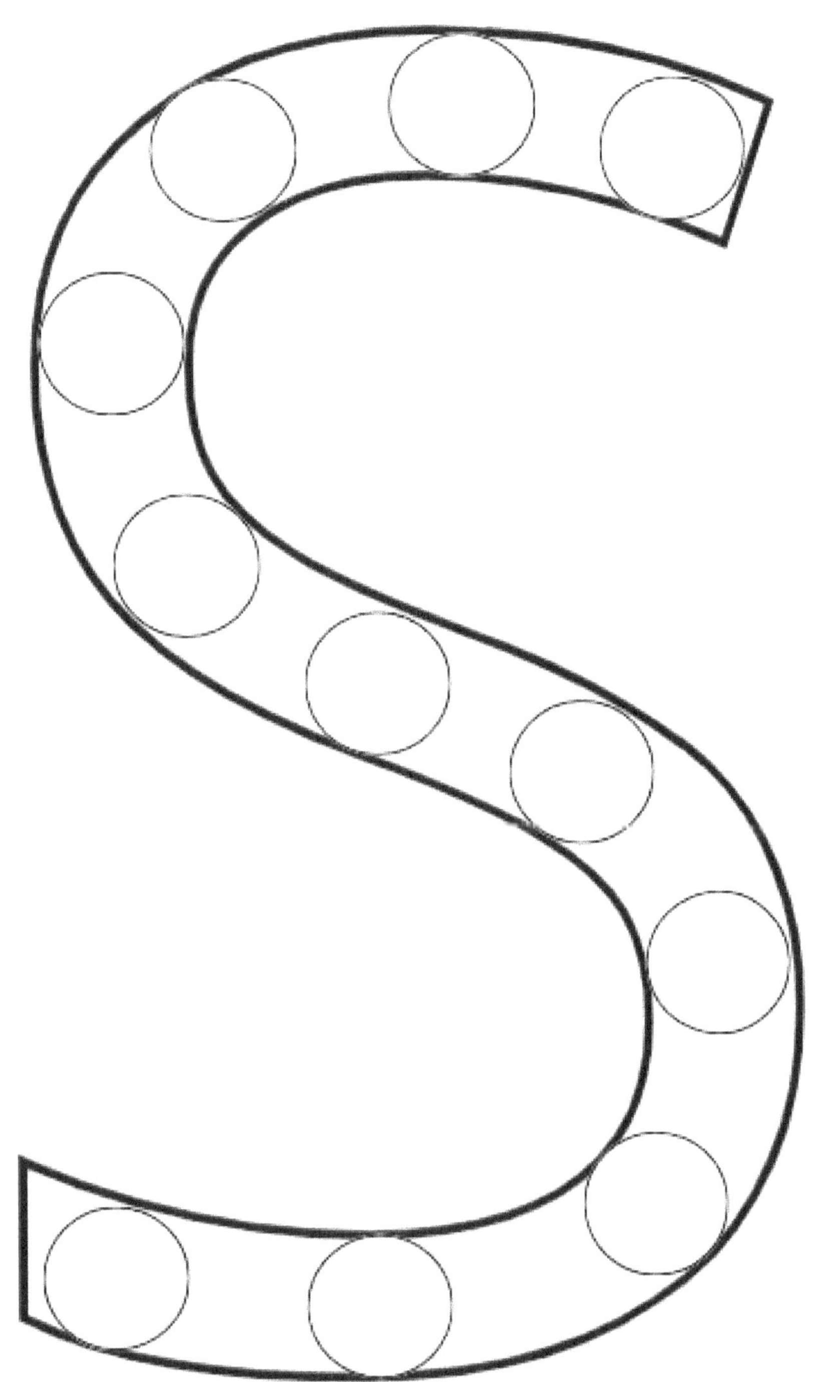

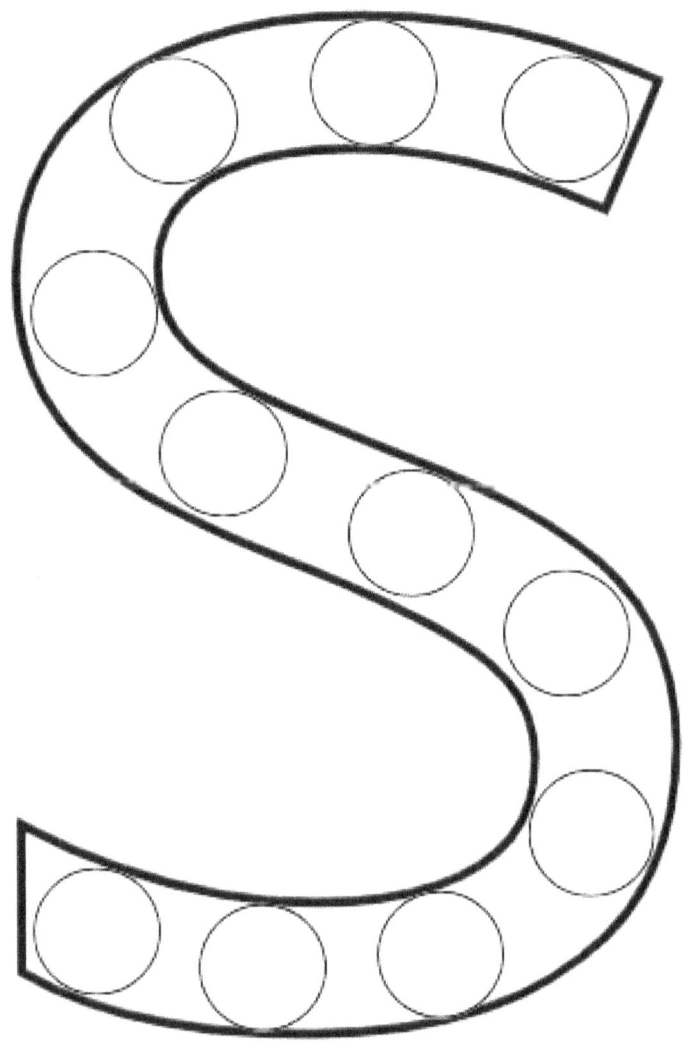

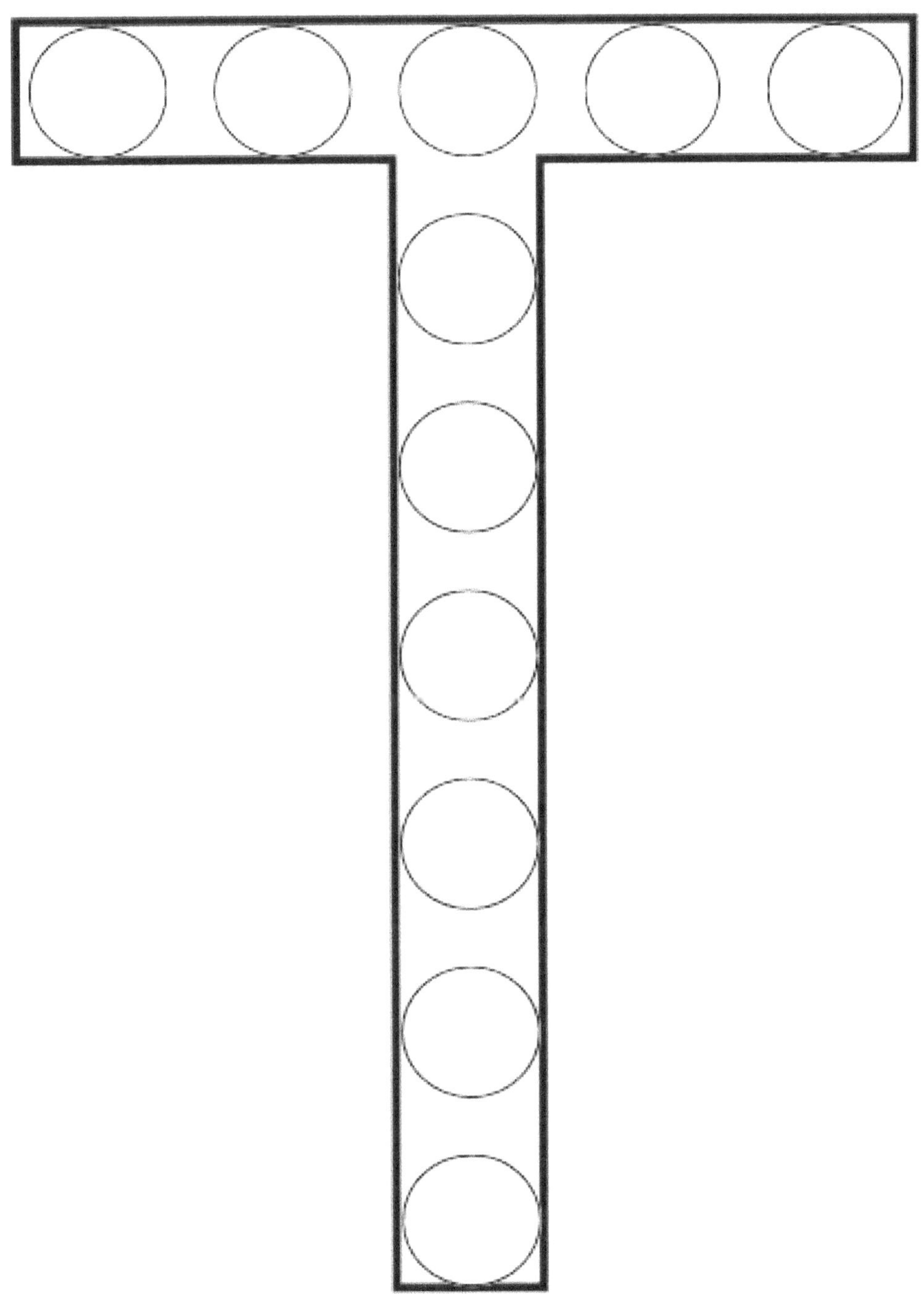

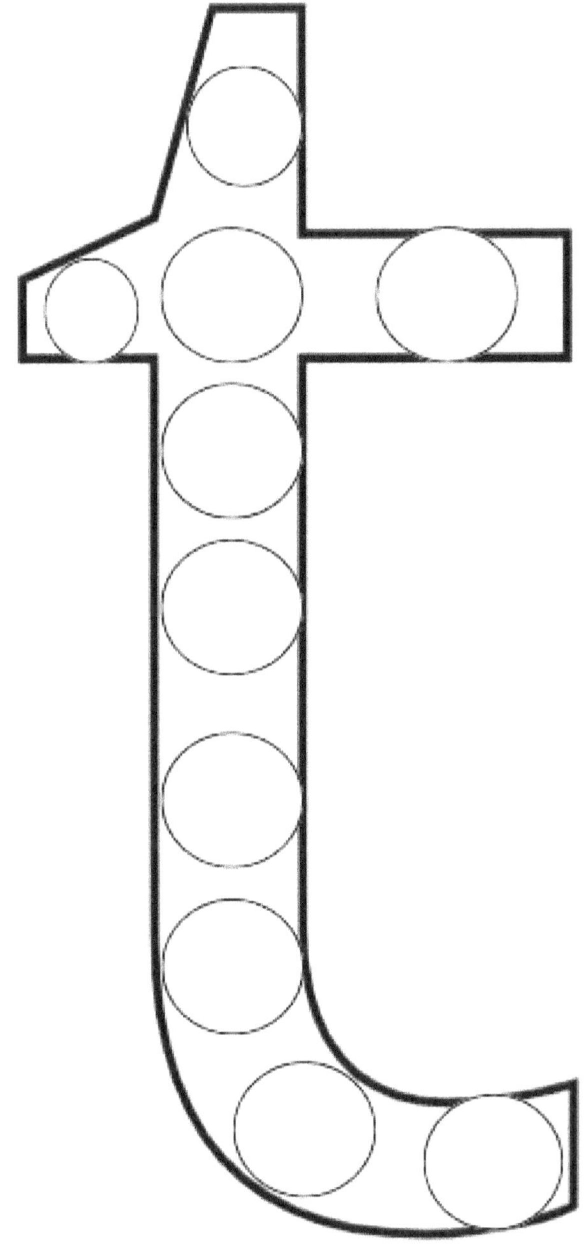

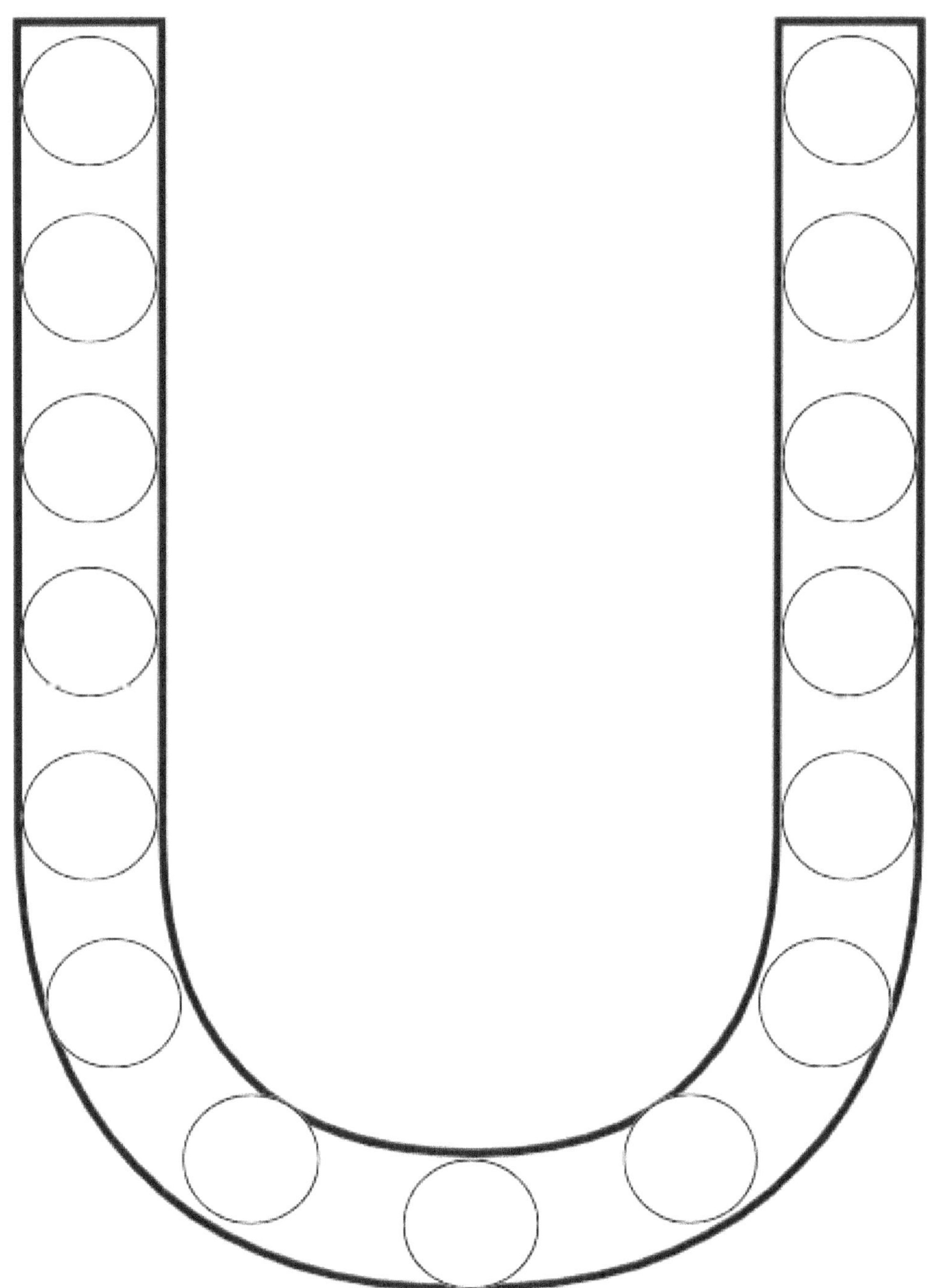

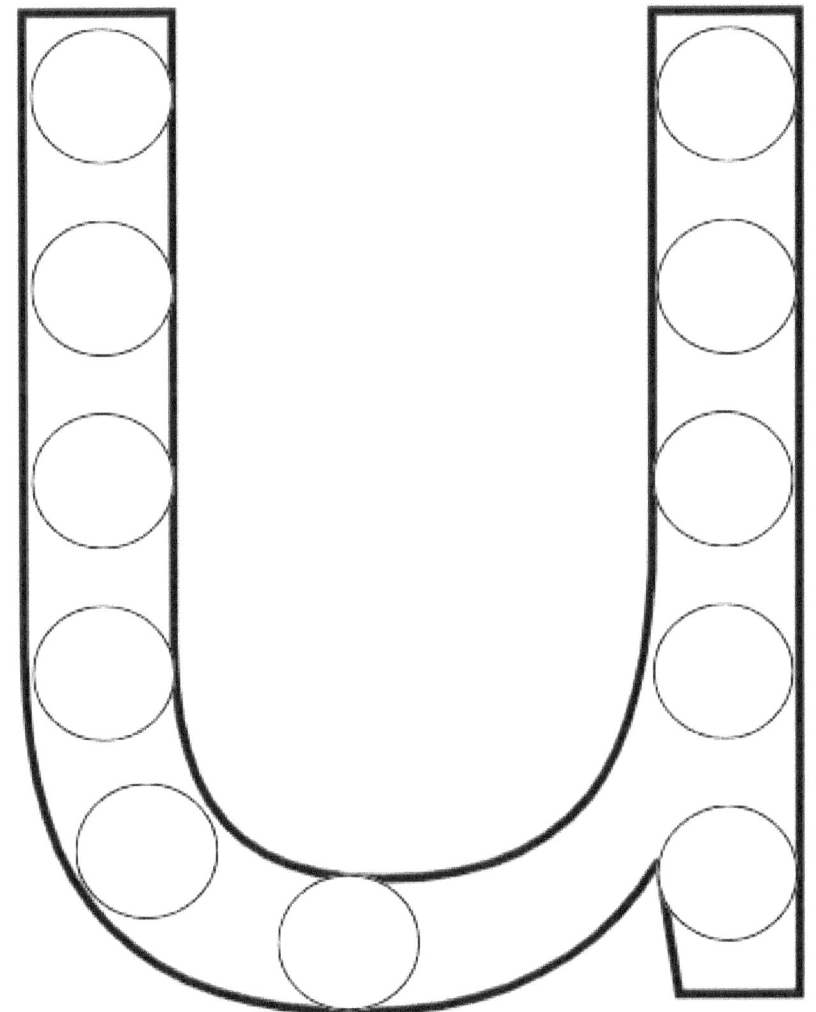

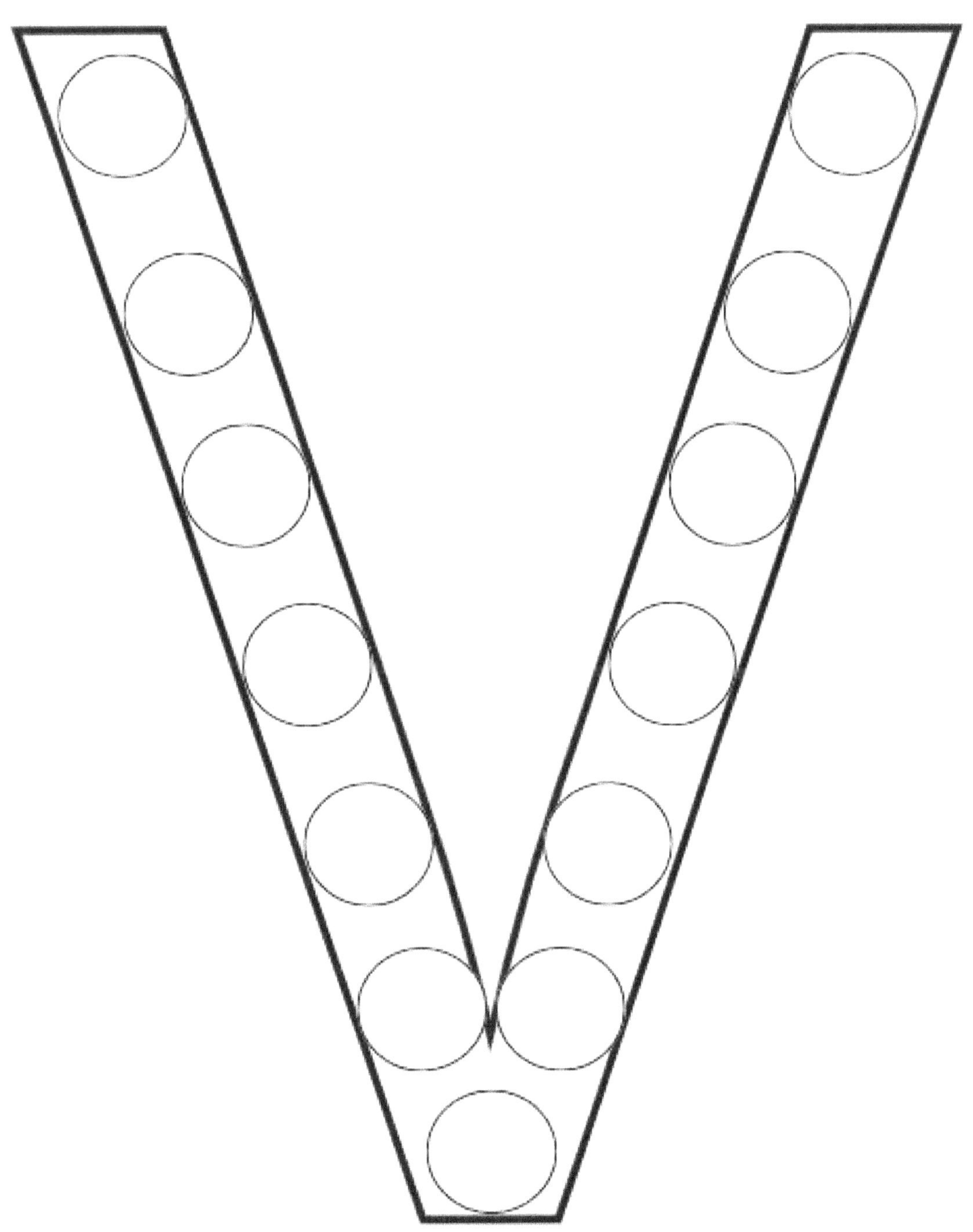

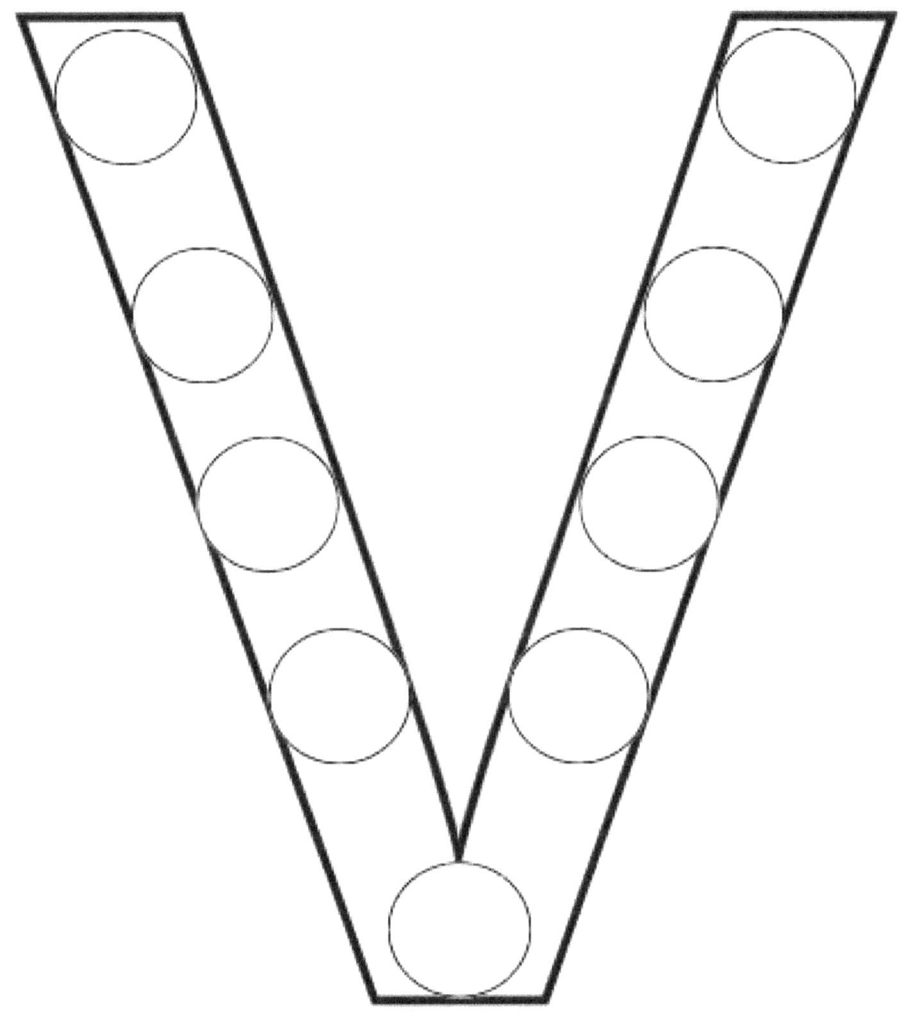

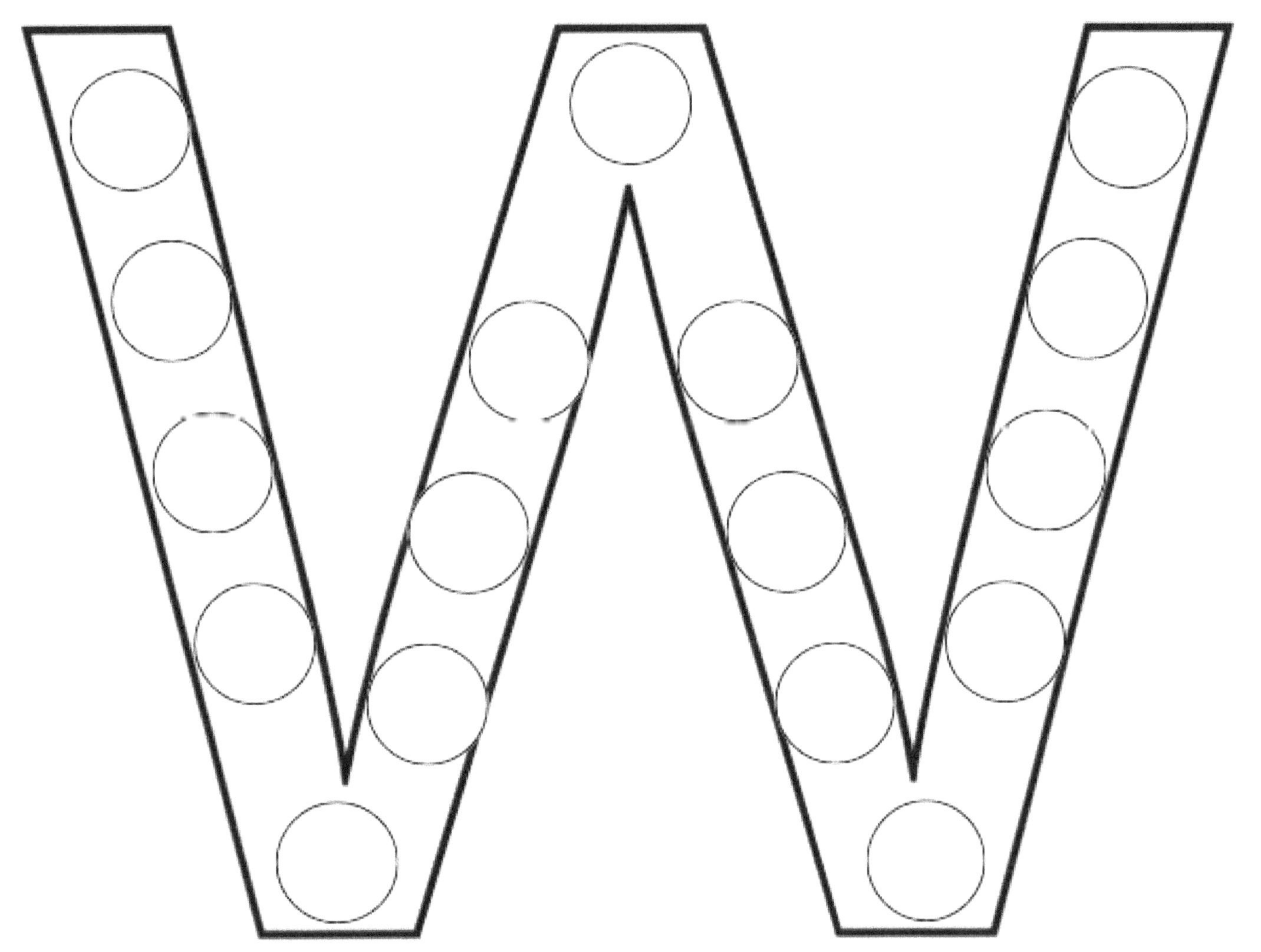

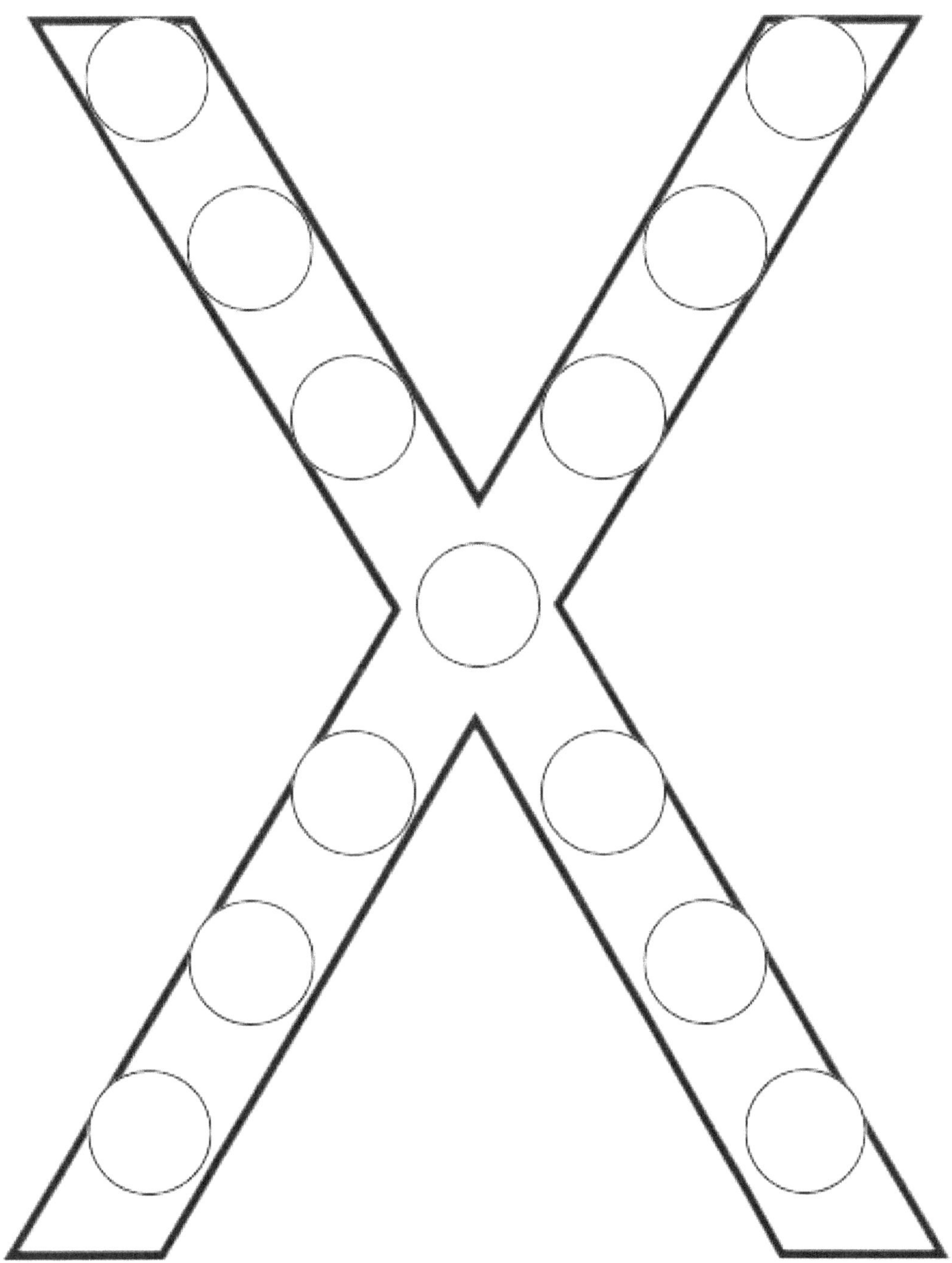

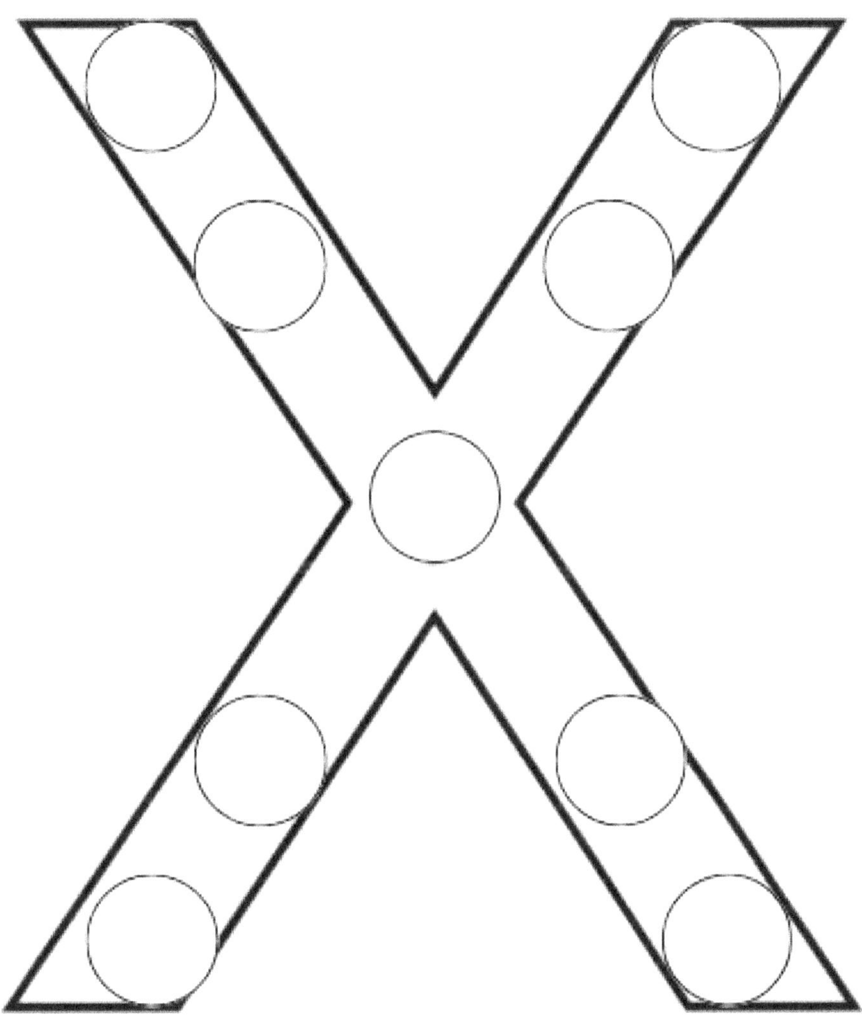

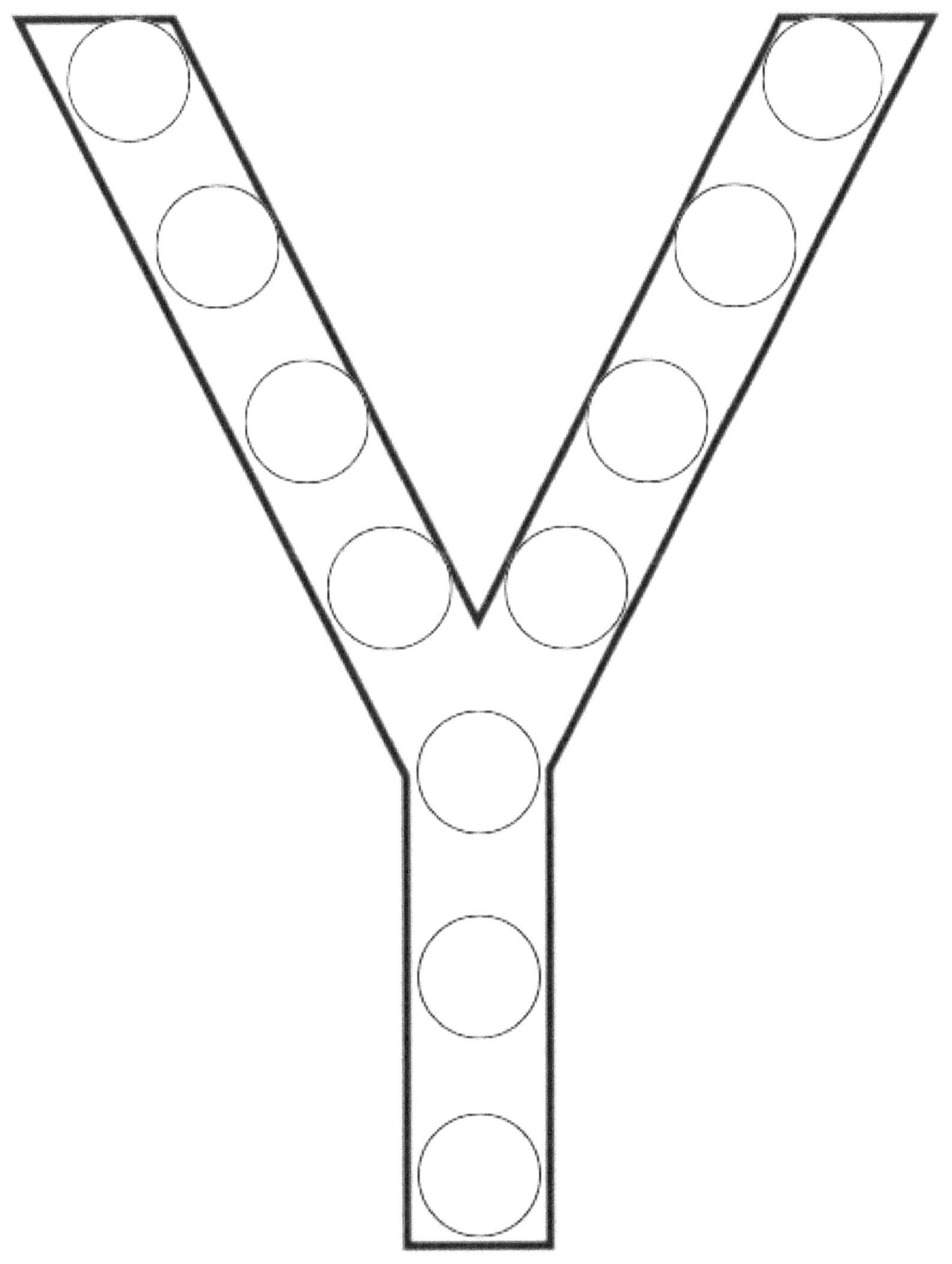

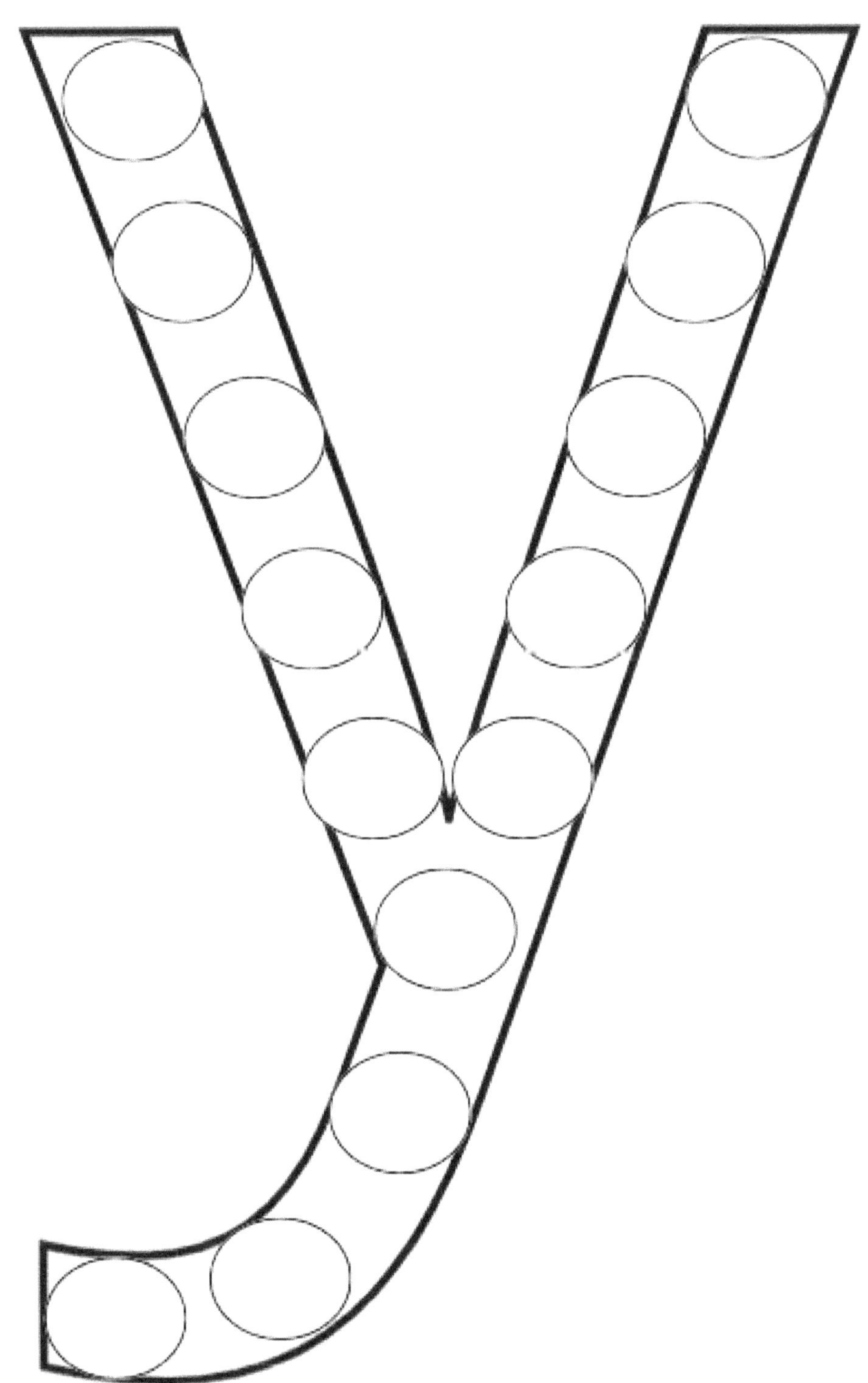

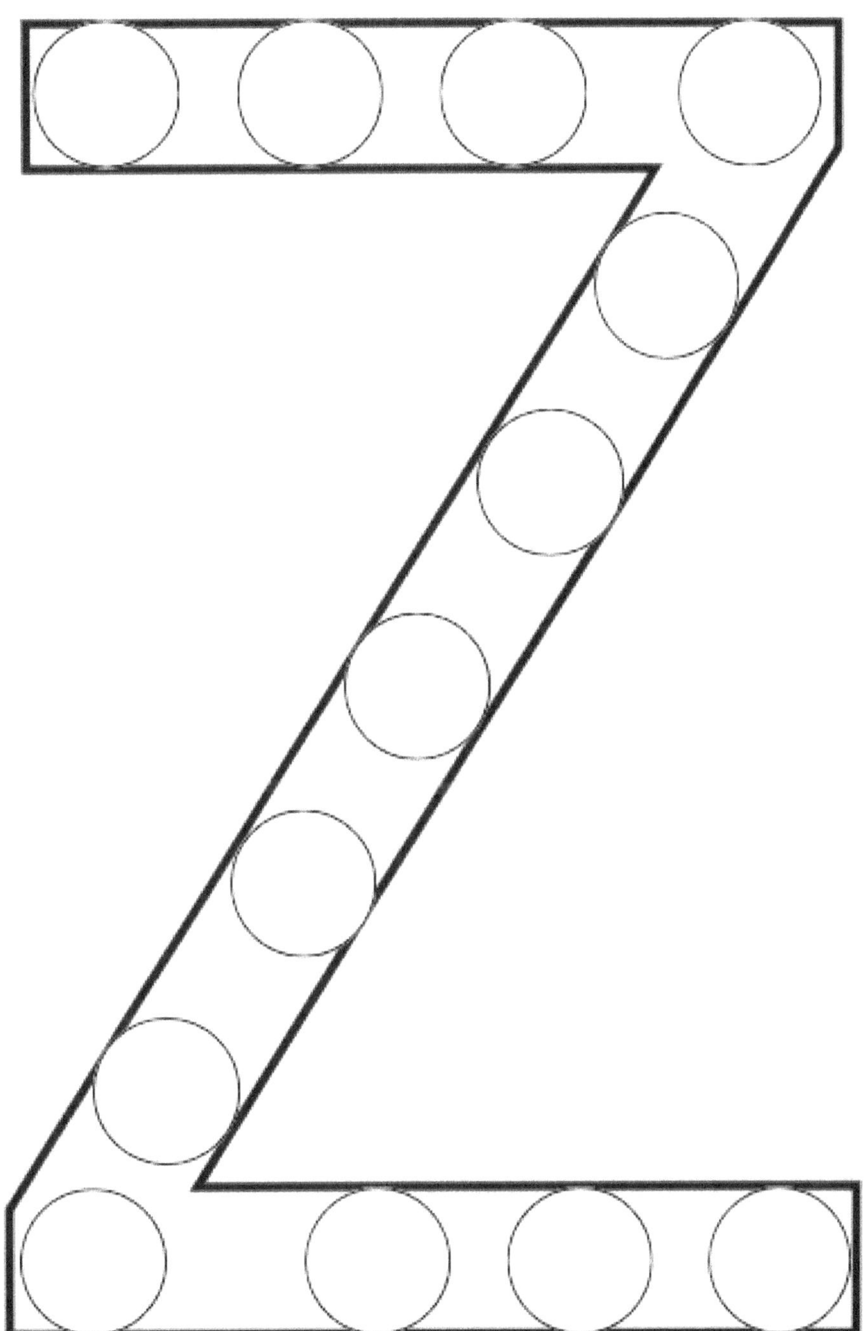

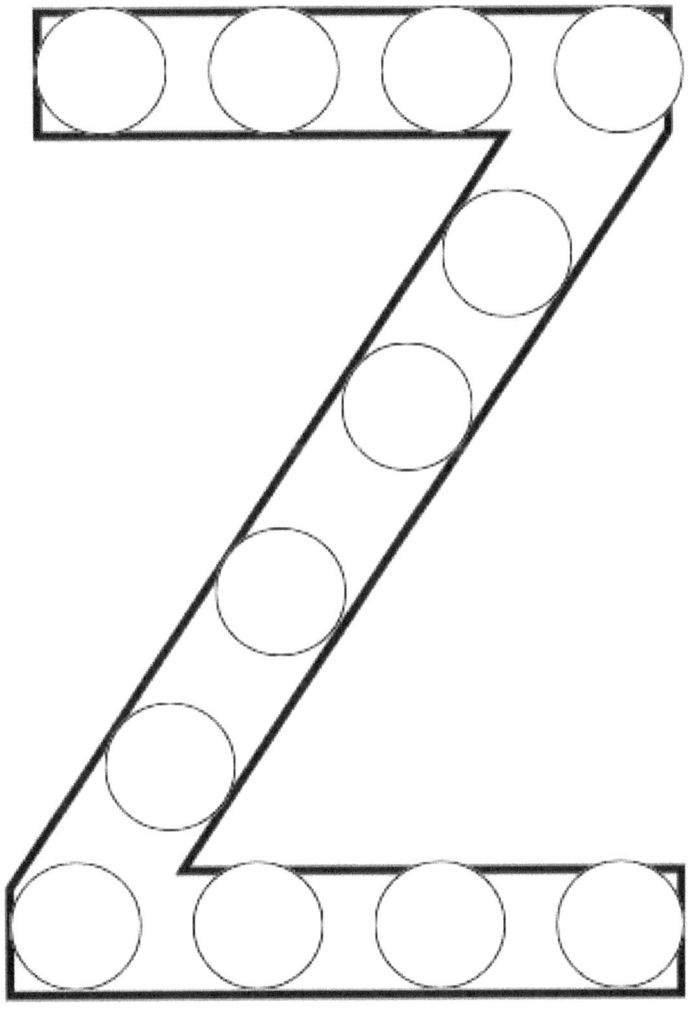